KU-003-302

Introduction

For years, the northern and eastern borders of the Soviet Union were well guarded by Mother Nature herself; the vast expanses of water and ice made them inaccessible for any foes. Things changed in the late 1940s with the advent of strategic bombers having intercontinental range. The development of a highly effective national air defence system capable of protecting the USSR from a possible NATO attack became a top-priority task, since the potential adversary possessed strategic bombers and cruise missiles capable of delivering one-megaton nuclear warheads that could destroy most of the nation's key industrial and military targets within a short time.

The first Soviet surface-to-air missile (SAM) systems had limited range and a kill altitude not exceeding 20,000 m (65,620 ft); thus, they were only good for point defence of key objectives. Conversely, missile-armed interceptors could destroy the attackers while these were still a long way from the Soviet borders, being an effective solution for covering the huge expanses of Siberia and the Soviet Far East where fielding a lot of SAMs was impossible. The first Soviet interceptors for the nation's Air Defence Force (PVO – *Protivovoz**doosh**naya obo**ro**na*) were developed in the late 1940s and early 1950s. By the mid-1950s, however, cannon-armed subsonic interceptors could no longer cope with high-flying and fast targets. Two approaches were pursued; the first was to equip production tactical fighters with airborne intercept radars and air-to-air missiles (AAMs), while the other option was to design dedicated interceptors from scratch, tailoring them to the PVO's needs. The interceptor was now regarded as part of an integrated aerial intercept weapons system comprising the aircraft itself (a missile platform), AAMs, a fire control radar and ground controlled intercept (GCI) systems. The first Soviet aerial intercept weapons systems to enter service were based on the subsonic Mikoyan/Gurevich MiG-17PFU (NATO reporting name *Fresco-E*) and Yakovlev Yak-25K *Flashlight-A*. Later the supersonic MiG-19PM *Farmer-E*, Sukhoi Su-9 *Fishpot-B* and Su-11 *Fishpot-C* were fielded nationwide, followed by the Su-15 *Flagon* and Yak-28P *Firebar*. However, these aircraft had an intercept range of several hundred kilometres at best. A totally new type of aircraft was required for intercepting targets at distances in excess of 1,000 km (620 miles) and altitudes in excess of 20,000 m (65,600 ft). The first attempt to create such an interceptor resulted in the Lavochkin La-250, which first flew on 16th July 1956. It had a design endurance of more than two hours in subsonic mode and a top speed of 1,600 km/h (990 mph). Yet the programme was plagued by accidents which, together with troublesome equipment and unsatisfactory handling, caused the trials to drag on for years and eventually led to the cancellation of the programme in 1959.

An early-model MiG-25P coded '07 Blue' carrying two R-40T IR-homing AAMs and two R-40R semi-active radar-homing AAMs.

A MiG-25PD ('75 Red') seen during trials, as indicated by the unusual orange colour of the R-40RD missile's wings; R-40TD AAMs are on the inboard pylons. The longer nose and the undernose FLIR housing (with a black anti-glare mask in front) are evident.

4000000002214 7

An operational MiG-25PD ('52 Blue') on quick-reaction alert with a full load of two R-40RDs inboard and four R-60 short-range IR-homing AAMs on APU-60-2 paired launchers outboard.

OKB-155 headed by Artyom I. Mikoyan (**opytno-konstrook**torskoye byu**ro** – experimental design bureau; the number is a code allocated for security reasons), which had made its mark as a 'fighter maker' in 1949 with the famous MiG-15 *Fagot*, was instructed to start work on superfast, ultra-high-flying heavy interceptors. In this context, 'heavy' means that the aircraft is larger and heavier than the 'light' interceptors adapted from tactical fighters and is designed for beyond visual range (BVR) combat, not for dogfighting. The first few of Mikoyan's 'heavy' fighters – the I-75, Ye-150 and particularly the Ye-152 series – were highly capable but did not progress beyond the prototype stage due to development problems and constantly changing requirements. (The Ye prefix means *yedinitsa* – 'unit', that is, 'one-off' aircraft.) Still, the Mikoyan OKB persevered. In February 1961 the Soviet Council of Ministers (= government) and the Communist Party Central Committee issued a joint directive tasking the OKB with developing an aircraft designated Ye-155 in interceptor and reconnaissance versions. Designed around two Tumanskiy R15B-300 afterburning turbojets with a reheat thrust of 10,150 kgp (22,380 lbst), the Ye-155P (*perekhvatchik* – interceptor) had a Smerch-A1 (Tornado-A1) radar with a detection range of 100 km (62.5 miles) and was armed with a quartet of R-40 medium-range AAMs – two semi-active radar-homing (SARH) R-40Rs and two IR-homing R-40Ts. The first prototype was completed in the summer of 1964, making its first flight on 9th September – six months after the Ye-155R (*razvedchik* – reconnaissance aircraft). In 1971 the interceptor entered production as the MiG-25P *Foxbat-A*. The Smerch-A1 radar (aka RP-25) could detect and track targets either autonomously or using ground inputs relayed via the **Vozdukh-1** (Air-1) GCI system. The *Lazoor'* (Prussian Blue) command link system connected with the radar allowed the aircraft to be directed to the target area automatically or semi-automatically.

Officially the MiG-25P entered service on 13th April 1972; by the mid-1970s it made up the backbone of the PVO's interceptor inventory. After converting to the MiG-25P, PVO units stationed near the borders successfully intercepted the USAF's Lockheed SR-71A spyplanes. In fact, the Blackbirds *could* have been shot down if need arose, and the only reason that they weren't that the actual order to fire was not given. At any rate, the SR-71s and Lockheed U-2s stayed away from the areas where MiG-25Ps were stationed.

After Lt. Viktor I. Belenko's infamous defection to Japan in a MiG-25P on 6th September 1976 the Soviet air defence force found itself in a predicament. Not only had the Americans studied the MiG-25P in detail, forcing the Mikoyan OKB to develop an urgent and massive upgrade as the MiG-25PD *Foxbat-E* with a new weapons control system (WCS), upgraded R-40TD/R-40RD missiles with almost twice the range, a new GCI system and a new identification friend-or-foe (IFF) system; Belenko had divulged that a new and far more capable two-seat version of the MiG-25 – tentatively designated 'Super *Foxbat*' by NATO but subsequently renamed *Foxhound* – was under development. This, in fact, was the aircraft which is the subject of this book – the MiG-31, the first Soviet fourth-generation fighter; a type which, alongside the Sukhoi Su-27P/Su-27SM *Flanker-B*, currently forms the backbone of Russia's air defence force.

Acknowledgements
The book is illustrated with photos by Yefim Gordon, Sergey Aleksandrov, Vitaliy Alyab'yev, Aleksandr Bel'tyukov, S. Gadzhi, Sergey Krivchikov, Sergey Kuznetsov, Aleksandr Melikhov, Vladimir Petrov, Dmitriy Pichugin, Il'ya Remeskov, Sergey Sergeyev, Maksim Skryabin, the late Sergey Skrynnikov, Valeriy Stepanchenko, Konstantin Tyurpeko, Andrey Zinchuk, Patrick Roegies, ITAR-TASS, as well as from the archive of RSK MiG, the personal archive of Yefim Gordon and from the following web sources: www.karopka.ru, www.scalemodels.ru, www.hyperscale.com, www.arcair.com, www.pienoismallit.net, www.modellversium.de, www.internetmodeler.com, www.russianplanes.net, Line drawings by Andrey Yurgenson. Colour drawings by Sergey Ignat'yev and Viktor Mil'yachenko.

From 'Bats' to 'Dogs'
The MiG-31 takes shape

As early as 1965, when the Ye-155P was in the midst of its test programme, the Mikoyan OKB was already considering a successor to this aircraft. The USSR had long been suffering from inadequate air defence of its northern regions. Airbases with good landing aids and powerful navigation facilities were few and far between in the High North. The existing network of air defence radars was capable of detecting low-flying targets only at close range. The MiG-25PD, Tupolev Tu-128 *Fiddler* and Sukhoi Su-15TM *Flagon-F* interceptors equipping the PVO units stationed up north were hampered by their limited range and WCS parameters. Therefore, the Mikoyan OKB proposed developing the MiG-25P into a long-range interceptor capable of patrolling alone over the northern wilderness and defending industrial centres effectively. The idea was supported by the government and the PVO command.

To this end the NII-339 avionics house (alias NIIR – *Na**ooch**no-is**sled**ovatel'skiy insti**toot rah**diostro**yen**iya*, Radio Equip-

ment Research Institute) had begun development of a new WCS based on the powerful Smerch-100 (Tornado-100) fire control radar, which was to work with the K-100 long-range AAM then under development at OKB-134. Yet by the end of the 1960s the Smerch-100 no longer met the current operational requirements. The potential adversary's offensive weapons systems were becoming increasingly more sophisticated, featuring new electronic countermeasures (ECM) equipment.

On 24th May 1968 the Council of Ministers issued a directive ordering the development of a new-generation aerial intercept system designated S-155. The directive tasked the Mikoyan OKB (which, after the death of its founder, was headed by Rostislav A. Belyakov) with designing and building reconnaissance, strike and interceptor versions of an aircraft designated Ye-155M; the latter version was designated **Ye-155MP** (*moderni**zee**rovannyy pere**khvat**chik* – updated interceptor). The aircraft was to

An early desktop model of the projected Ye-155MP featuring variable-geometry wings (shown here at maximum sweep), tandem cockpits and four-wheel main gear bogies.

A slightly different model of the 'swing-wing' Ye-155MP (note the longer nose) with the wings at minimum sweep; note the large ventral fins which were to fold inwards when the gear was down.

A comparison of two VG-wing Ye-155MP configurations having tandem seating and side-by-side seating.

Lower views of the same models showing the different placement of the long-range (K-100 AAMs under the fuselage and the wing gloves or K-33s in a diamond arrangement under the fuselage); neither arrangement was accepted. Note that the 'side-by-side' version has one ventral fin, not two.

have a cruising speed of about 3,000 km/h (1,864 mph) and be capable of destroying multiple targets in a single sortie. In keeping with the development schedule set out in the directive the aircraft was to commence state acceptance (= certification) trials in the fourth quarter of 1971.

The PVO's specific operational requirement for the new interceptor demanded, above all, an increase in range and endurance (on-station loiter time); on the other hand, the speed and service ceiling target figures were almost unchanged as compared to the MiG-25P. The aircraft was to have a maximum interception range of 700 km (434 miles) when cruising at 2,500 km/h (1,552 mph) or Mach 2.35; at subsonic speed the maximum interception range was extended to 1,200 km (745 miles).

The envisaged automated data link/tactical information exchange system was to enable groups of fighters to protect the vast stretches of Soviet territory in the High North and Far East lacking adequate radar coverage. Realising the high complexity of the WCS, the military consented to a crew of two – a pilot and a navigator/weapons systems officer (WSO). It would be utterly impossible for a single pilot to fly the aircraft while monitoring the tactical situation, monitoring the aircraft's systems and taking decisions whether to attack the target or not; the WSO would take over some of these functions, allowing the pilot to concentrate on the flying.

One of the crucial requirements was the ability to destroy low-flying cruise missiles at long range. The reason was that the cruise missiles could be equipped with nuclear war-

This desktop model of the Ye-155MP has fixed-geometry wings featuring large LERXes which were to be raised into position as required – a unique feature.

heads, and a possible detonation of such a warhead would wipe out the attacking interceptor or SAM site at several miles' range.

At the Mikoyan OKB the interceptor bore the in-house code *iz**del**iye* (product) 518. Three alternative general arrangements were considered at the preliminary design (PD) stage. Some of the many project versions progressed as far as the advanced development project (ADP) stages, and thus merit a brief description; they differed mainly in wing and vertical tail design, the fuselage shape and the MiG-25's distinctively raked two-dimensional lateral air intakes with horizontal airflow control ramps remaining virtually unchanged.

One of the first Ye-155MP design studies featured **variable-geometry (VG) wings**, looking like a cross between the MiG-23 *Flogger* and the MiG-25. In one version the pilot and WSO sat in tandem cockpits under a common canopy strongly reminiscent of the McDonnell Douglas F-4 Phantom II; another had side-by-side seating in the manner of the General Dynamics F-111 Aardvark. The shoulder-mounted wings and the single vertical tail with a prominent fillet were quite similar to those of the MiG-23; one version featured two large ventral fins to ensure directional stability, the fins folding when the landing gear was extended – again in similar manner to the MiG-23. The main landing gear units were unusual in having four-wheel bogies to reduce runway loading,

enabling the aircraft to operate from semi-prepared strips (this was later changed to two wheels in tandem); the nose unit had twin wheels. The armament consisted of three or four K-33 long-range AAMs which, for the first time on a Soviet fighter, were semi-recessed in the fuselage underside; short-range AAMs could be carried on pylons under the fixed wing gloves. The VG wings improved field performance and increased on-station loiter time in certain flight modes. However, they incurred a weight penalty and increased structural complexity; besides, unlike the MiG-23, the Ye-155MP was not intended for dogfighting where 'swing wings' might confer an advantage, so this project version was soon abandoned.

A version bearing the in-house designation *izdeliye* **518-21** was proposed in 1968. However, it soon became apparent that the aircraft would be overweight and short on rate of climb and service ceiling; hence development of this version was discontinued. The *izdeliye* **518-22** project version followed in 1969; it had fixed-geometry trapezoidal wings, MiG-25 style twin tails and, again, tandem seating for the crew and semi-recessed carriage of the K-33 missiles in tandem pairs. The wings had a three-spar structure instead of the *Foxbat*'s two-spar structure for added torsional stiffness and featured prominent leading-edge root extensions (LERXes) and leading-edge flaps. The landing gear was totally reworked, the for-

The very similar *izdeliye* 518-22 project configuration with the LERXes raised.

ward-retracting main units featuring twin-wheel bogies with smaller wheels to cater for the higher all-up weight. The wheels on each bogie had a staggered-tandem arrangement, the front wheel being located inboard and the rear wheel outboard. The forward main-wheel well doors doubled as airbrakes. The twin-wheel nose unit retracted aft, not forward as on the MiG-25. These features were later incorporated in the Ye-155MP's definitive project form.

Other PD project versions of the Ye-155MP included **izdeliye 518-31**, of which no details are available, and **izdeliye**

518-55, which combined the forward and centre fuselage of the eventual MiG-31 with the tail unit of the MiG-25, except that the wings were more like those of the MiG-29 *Fulcrum* light fighter. The most unconventional version bore a separate designation, **Ye-158**, utilising a tailless-delta layout with ogival wings of increased area. One might also mention the **Ye-155MF** (*frontovoy* – frontline, that is, tactical), a bomber derivative with the two crew members seated side-by-side in similar manner to the Sukhoi Su-24 *Fencer* tactical bomber (to which it lost out) to give the navigator/WSO a better field of view.

The *izdeliye* 518-55 project configuration shows the new wings with compound curvature not unlike those of the MiG-29.

This view of the *izdeliye* 518-55 model shows the tandem pairs of K-33 AAMs (the arrangement eventually accepted) and the tandem-wheel main gear bogies. Note also the folded ventral fin with a dielectric bottom portion.

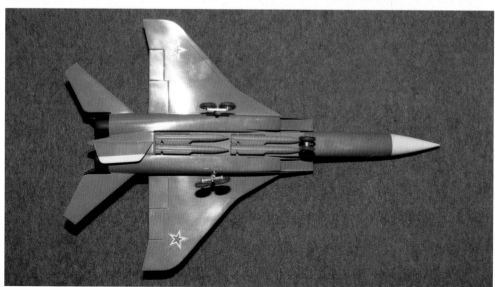

Full-scale design work on the Ye-155MP began in 1972 under the guidance of chief project engineer Gleb Ye. Lozino-Lozinskiy. In the course of detail design the Ye-155MP drifted steadily away from the MiG-25 until eventually all they had in common was the general arrangement and, more or less, the basic dimensions. Suffice it to say that the share of high-strength stainless steel, titanium and aluminium alloys in the Ye-155MP's airframe was 50%, 16% and 33%, whereas on the MiG-25 this proportion was 80%, 8% and 11% respectively.

Here we should turn our attention to what was packed inside the Ye-155MP's airframe. At a very early stage, in order to meet the range and endurance requirements coupled with ensuring adequate speed performance, it was decided – for the first time in Soviet fighter design practice – to equip the Ye-155MP with afterburning turbofans. The chosen engine was the D30F-6 developed by OKB-19 under Pavel A. Solov'yov in Perm'; it was a thorough rework of the 6,800-kgp (14,990-lbst) D-30 Srs 2 commercial turbofan powering the Tupolev Tu-134A/Tu-134B *Crusty* short-haul airliner. The F suffix stood for *for**see**rovannyy* – uprated, by replacing the thrust reverser with an afterburner and making other changes the OKB managed to obtain a maximum thrust of 15,500 kgp (34,170 lbst). The turbofan offered much better fuel efficiency than contemporary Soviet fighter engines, especially in subsonic flight modes.

Development of the D30F-6 likewise began in 1972. Three years later the engine was put through its paces on two extensively modified *Foxbats* (a MiG-25P and a MiG-25RB *Foxbat-A* reconnaissance aircraft) known as the *izdeliye* 99 engine testbeds on which both turbojets were replaced by D30F-6s and the inlet ducts widened to cater for the greater mass flow. The engine entered production in 1976, passing state acceptance trials in 1979.

To ensure stable engine operation in all flight modes and optimise the fuel flow the engine control system included a digital control unit; it was effectively the first Soviet full authority digital engine control (FADEC) system ensuring more precise fuel flow control than traditional hydromechanical fuel control units (FCUs), with due regard to such variables as altitude, Mach number, kinetic heating of the airframe, engine rpm and engine air pressure. The BSP-48 surge prevention system automatically throttled back the affected engine in the event of surge; it also automatically activated the igniters and the oxygen supply if the engine ran roughly or flamed out. The system was activated by the surge sensor and by the missile launch commands given by the crew.

Initially NII-339 was tasked with developing the Ye-155MP's new-generation weapons control system. However, the establishment was overburdened with current high-priority programmes, and the new assignment was more than it could handle; therefore the Ministry of Electronics Industry decided to merge this establishment with the Zhukovskiy-based OKB-15 in order to pool resources. The resulting entity named NPO Fazotron (*na**ooch**no-proiz**vod**stvennoye obyedi**nen**iye* – 'Phasotron' Scientific & Production Association) set to work developing a new multi-channel long-range aerial intercept system designated S-800 *Za**slon** (Shield, or Barrier). NPO Fazotron was assigned overall responsibility for the WCS, including the radar and the semi-active radar seeker head of the K-33 long-range AAM – the future interceptor's main weapon. Integration of the system's components was the domain of the State Research Institute for Aircraft Systems (Gos-NII AS – *Gosu**dar**stvennyy na**ooch**no-iss**sle**dovatel'skiy insti**toot** aviatsion**nykh sistem**).

The design philosophy of the Zaslon system was markedly different from that of its US counterparts. The emphasis was placed on the ability to operate independently, long intercept range and the ability to protect large areas, and multi-channel targeting capability plus multiple threat attack capability. Since the Ye-155MP was to be armed with four K-33 missiles, the objective was to give it the ability to attack four targets at once. Since priority threats had to be identified and attacked first, the number of simultaneously tracked targets had to be greater than four – that is, the radar had track-while-scan capability, which contemporary radars with mechanically scanned antennas lacked. The maximum number of targets (ten) was determined by the sum of the time periods needed for tracking each target and by the scan time. The width of the scanned area was to ensure coverage of a zone 200 km (124 miles) wide measured at the radar horizon. Detection range against a target with a radar cross-section (RCS) of 19 m² (204.3 sq ft) – which matches that of the SR-71, one of the toughest targets to intercept – was to be 180-200 km (111-124 miles), several times longer than for any existing Soviet interceptor type. Maximum tracking range for a bomber-sized target was to be 120 km (74.5 miles); maximum tracking range for a fighter-sized target was to be 90 km (55.9 miles) in head-on mode and 70 km (43.5 miles) in pursuit mode. The Zaslon WCS was to enable concerted action by a flight of interceptors when target information was intermittent or limited to a single report; this would allow the aircraft to operate in areas with only partial radar coverage.

After analysing the options, in 1969 the designers of the WCS opted for a phased-array radar with a fixed antenna and an electronically scanned beam. This was a 'world's first' – such systems had not been used hitherto on fighters and the task was extremely complex. A lengthy quest by trial and error followed as various engineering solutions were tested; it was not until 1975 that a satisfactory phased-array antenna – the fourth version developed – was available for testing.

For the first time in the world the N007 fire control radar (known as RP-31 or *izdeliye*

A model of the projected Ye-155MF strike version having side-by-side seating and armed with four Kh-58 anti-radar missiles on the wing pylons.

8B in production form; NATO codename *Flash Dance*) incorporated a three-channel (search, tracking and IFF) antenna system and a digital processor with narrow-band Doppler filtration. Other 'firsts' for a Soviet interceptor included pulse-Doppler data processing, continuous sampling target illumination, a tactical information display and a digital data processing system based on the A-15 (Argon-15) mainframe computer. The latter, an 'off-the-shelf' component, was not particularly fast; yet it was the only indigenous compact digital processor available at the time, so it was basically 'take it or leave it'. On the other hand, the phased-array antenna of 1.1 m (3 ft 7⁵⁄₁₆ in) diameter was something of a 'golden standard' as far as the basic emission parameters are concerned. It was the world's first radar working in two wavebands (X-band and L-band); in effect, it featured separate phased arrays, one for each waveband, giving a scan angle of ±60°. (It should be noted that the first Western fighters to feature phased-array radars entered production in the 21st century, when the subject of this book had been in service for two decades.) As compared to the RP-23 *Sapfeer-23* (Sapphire-23) fire control radar fitted to the MiG-23M *Flogger-B*, the new radar offered twice the detection range. Priority targets were designated automatically (in accordance with the parameters entered into the computer) or manually by the crew.

The main difficulties encountered in designing the radar included ensuring the required low noise level for the transmitter and wide dynamic range for the receiver. Seven variants of the phased-array antenna were developed and tested consecutively; the theoretical principles of phased-array antenna design were evolved in parallel. A major problem that had to be solved was that the transmitter's signal lay within the receiver's Doppler range, creating false radar returns. Another problem was that the powerful vacuum tubes used in the radar set turned out to be rather troublesome. Four versions of the radar transmitter had to be tested until the results were satisfactory.

The data processing system of the Zaslon WCS featured a digital databus linking the mainframe computer with all other components of the weapons control system – for the first time on a Soviet fighter. The ability to guide other fighters with less sophisticated radars to their targets was implemented. Other advanced combat functions included the possibility of two interceptors simultaneously attacking a top-priority threat and the possibility of transferring the guidance of a missile fired by one interceptor to another aircraft.

To increase the chances of a 'kill' in an ECM environment the designers of the Zaslon WCS supplemented the radar with an infra-red search & track (IRST) unit. This system (designated *izdeliye* 8TK in production form, TK probably standing for *teplovoy kanahl* [*sistemy navedeniya*] – thermal [targeting system] channel) was developed by TsKB *Gheofizika* ('Geophysics' Central Design Bureau) led by D. M. Khorol in 1970. It allowed the interceptor to launch a stealthy attack in pursuit mode without revealing itself by switching on the radar. It was assumed that, once the aircraft had been guided to the target by a GCI system, the IRST would detect the target and track it with sufficient accuracy for an attack with IR-homing missiles.

It was envisaged that the IRST unit would only be used at high altitude; hence the unit was housed in a retractable cylindrical pod that was normally stowed in the forward fuselage underside. A set of revolving mirrors focused the thermal image on a heat sensor cooled by liquid nitrogen. The *izdeliye* 8TK commenced bench testing in 1977; target tracking dynamics and infra-red countermeasures (IRCM) resistance were assessed, including the ability to discern between the real target and IRCM decoys.

The Zaslon WCS was put through its paces on two Tupolev Tu-104 *Camel* twinjet medium-haul airliners converted into LM-104-518 avionics testbeds by NPO Vzlyot (Take-off), another avionics house. The radar was installed in a large conical radome supplanting the glazed navigator's station in the Tu-104's nose. The first aircraft (CCCP-42324), which entered flight test in the spring of 1973, was used to perfect the radar's beam scanning function and refining the target detection and tracking process. The second testbed (CCCP-42454), which first flew in the autumn of 1975, was mostly intended for verifying the WCS as a whole. It also served for integration of the K-33 missiles' seeker heads with the radar; to this end it was fitted with missile pylons from which inert K-33s were actually launched, and was thus the world's only airliner armed with missiles! Fast jets (a MiG-21 *Fishbed* fighter and a MiG-25P) were also modified in 1970 and 1973 respectively as avionics/weapons testbeds for the Zaslon suite.

The missile itself was developed by MKB **Vym**pel (*ma**shin**ostro**itel**'noye kon**strook**torskoye by**uro** – 'Pennant' Machinery Design Bureau), formerly OKB-134, which was then headed by Andrey L. Lyapin. The K-33 featured short strake-like wings and folding rudders; this allowed the missile to be carried semi-recessed in the fuselage underside, cutting the aircraft's overall drag considerably. During launch the missiles were to be propelled clear of the aircraft by AKU-410 pantographic ejector racks before the rocket motor was ignited. The K-33's airframe made large-scale use of titanium alloys; the launch weight was 491 kg (1,082 lb), including a 55-kg (121-lb) warhead. The maximum effective 'kill' range was 130 km (80.75 miles); the missile was to be effective against targets flying at altitudes of 50-28,000 m (164-91,860 ft) and speeds up to 3,700 km/h (2,300 mph) and the 'kill' probability against a target making 4-G evasive manoeuvres was 60-80%.

In addition to the four underfuselage racks, two 'wet' hardpoints were provided under the wings; these could carry short-range or medium-range IR-homing AAMs or two 2,500-litre (550 Imp gal) drop tanks. For close-in combat the Ye-155MP was armed with a 23-mm (.90 calibre) Gryazev/Shipunov GSh-6-23 six-barrel Gatling cannon with 260 rounds. Its normal rate of fire was 6,000 rounds per minute and could be increased to 8,000 rpm in case of need. The cannon was to be mounted on the starboard air intake trunk, just aft of the main landing gear unit.

The interceptor's navigation suite included the SAU-155MP automatic control system (*sistem**a** avtoma**tich**eskovo oo**prav**l**eniy**a*) and the KN-25 integrated navigation system (*kompleks navigatsion**nyy***). The latter consisted of the following components: two IS-1-72A inertial navigation systems, a *Man**yovr*** (Manoeuvre) digital processor, an A-312 *Radi**kal**-NP* short-range radio navigation system (SHORAN), an A-723 *Kvi**tok-2*** (Receipt-2) long-range radio navigation system (LORAN), and Tropik and *Marsh**root*** (Route) global positioning system receivers. A defensive avionics suite comprising ECM and active/passive IRCM gear for protection against missile attack was also envisaged.

The designers of the K-33 missile and the aircraft's navigation and targeting suite had to tackle a host of engineering problems. A peculiarity of the K-33 system was that the missile had inertial guidance during the initial phase of the flight (up to 20% of the trajectory length) with mid-course heading correction until the radar seeker head achieved a lock-on at the terminal guidance phase; this guidance algorithm was a 'world first'. Thus, guidance accuracy was affected not only by the operation of the radar seeker head but also by inertial navigation system (INS) errors, which depended a lot on the accuracy of the launch point co-ordinates fed into the INS. These, in turn, were affected by the error margins of the aircraft's navigation and targeting suite, which needed to be minimised. To complicate matters further, the problems associated with navigation in the Polar regions had to be taken into account. The Ye-155MP's required long endurance created another stumbling block: INS accuracy was directly affected by the period of its operation; as time passed, the INS started generating errors which sometimes could not be corrected by means of celestial or satellite navigation. This called for high-precision primary data sensors (gyros and accelerometers) to ensure the required accuracy. Sure enough, the designers managed to sort out all of these often conflicting requirements, but as a result the navigation suite turned out to be not only effective but highly complex as well.

Like all contemporary Soviet tactical aircraft, the Ye-155MP was to be equipped with K-36D Srs 2 'zero-zero' ejection seats developed and produced by NPP *Zvez**da*** ('Star' Scientific & Production Enterprise, formerly OKB-918) led by Guy I. Severin.

Thus by the mid-1970s the multitude of aircraft industry, electronics industry and defence industry enterprises involved in the S-155 programme had completed the entire scope of research and development work on the aircraft and its systems. In its ideology and performance the S-155 aerial intercept system comprising the Ye-155MP heavy interceptor, the Zaslon WCS and the K-33 AAM had no direct counterpart in the outside world and excelled contemporary Western aircraft.

The B1.01M phased array of the N007 radar developed for the Ye-155MP.

The Kennel
Foxhound Versions

The detail design stage lasted several years; Mikoyan OKB General Designer Rostislav A. Belyakov exercised overall control of the Ye-155MP programme. At this stage the interceptor received a new in-house product code, *izdeliye* 83, and the provisional service designation **MiG-25MP** (which proved to be short-lived). It was a two-seat fourth-generation aircraft with enhanced capabilities as compared to the MiG-25P/PD, even though the latter had a higher top speed and service ceiling. Its mission was to intercept high- and low-flying agile and non-agile targets (including those flying at ultra-low altitude) in head-on and pursuit mode while travelling at high supersonic speeds. The aircraft was to be capable of doing this around the clock, in any weather and in an ECM environment. The addition of a WSO not only facilitated the operation of the more complex weapons system but also eased the psychological strain on the pilot during long patrol missions, especially overwater flights – the pilot no longer felt he was 'all alone over the briny'. Additionally, the rear cockpit was provided with a telescopic control stick, rudder pedals and a pop-up forward vision periscope, obviating the need for a trainer version.

The result of these efforts was an aircraft with unmatched capabilities. Despite its apparent similarity to the MiG-25P/PD, the new aircraft was different in virtually every aspect, be it aerodynamics (which were more refined), structural design, powerplant, armament or avionics. The fuselage and air intake trunks contributed a sizeable amount of lift – as much as 50% in some flight modes. The relatively thin wings were cambered to delay the onset of tip stall at high angles of attack in subsonic mode and featured small LERXes that enhanced manoeuvrability at high AOAs. The wings featured four-section leading-edge flaps increasing lift in loiter mode; the trailing edge was occupied by two-section flaps and ailerons. To improve the lift/drag ratio in subsonic cruise, the LE and TE flaps were set 13° and 5° respectively, the ailerons drooping 5° at the same time.

The landing gear with its unorthodox staggered-tandem mainwheels allowed the bogies to somersault during retraction, folding into the smallest possible space; another bonus was the dramatically reduced runway loading, which allowed the interceptor to operate from *ad hoc* semi-prepared runways.

'831 Blue', the first of two Ye-155MP prototypes, in the assembly shop of the Mikoyan OKB's prototype manufacturing plant (MMZ No.155).

Quite apart from the host of technical problems encountered while developing the aircraft, its engines and radar, the designers had to cut through miles of bureaucratic red tape. All this caused prototype construction to be delayed. At a conference of the PVO' top command in 1975 it was pointed out that in spite of the 33 (!) government directives concerning the MiG-25MP issued to date, the aircraft still hadn't entered service.

The two prototypes were built at the Mikoyan OKB's experimental production facility, MMZ No.155 (*Moskovskiy mashinostroitel'nyy zavod* – Moscow Machinery Plant). Appropriately coded '831 Blue' (that is, *izdeliye 83/1*, as it was known in-house), the first prototype was rolled out in mid-1975. It lacked the radar (which was substituted by test equipment), some other avionics items and the cannon. As originally built the aircraft had stock MiG-25RB wing panels with no LE flaps and no LERXes (the intended wings with leading-edge devices and drooping ailerons were retrofitted later); it also had the older KM-1M ejection seats instead of the envisaged K-36DM seats.

On 16th September 1975 the first prototype made its successful maiden flight with Mikoyan OKB chief test pilot Aleksandr V. Fedotov, Hero of the Soviet Union, at the con-

trols and V. S. Zaïtsev in the back seat; the manufacturer's flight tests began. One by one, Mikoyan OKB test pilots Pyotr M. Ostapenko, Boris A. Orlov, Aviard G. Fastovets, Valeriy Ye. Menitskiy and Toktar O. Aubakirov joined the flight test programme. The second prototype, '832 Blue' (*izdeliye 83/2*), was completed with a full avionics fit and a full armament system, making its first flight in May 1976 at the hands of Pyotr M. Stefanovskiy; at the end of the year it was turned over to the Soviet Air Force's Red Banner State Research Institute named after Valeriy P. Chkalov (GNIKI VVS – *Gosudarstvennyy naoochno-issledovatel'skiy Krasnoznamyonnyy instittoot Voyenno-vozdooshnykh seel*; the 'Red Banner' bit denotes an award of the Red Banner of Combat Order) to commence state acceptance trials.

So great was the government's faith in the Ye-155MP (which would undoubtedly be superior to all of the PVO's then-current interceptors) that the interceptor was ordered into production at aircraft factory No. 21 named after Sergo Ordzhonikidze in Gor'kiy – the plant producing the MiG-25 – as early as 10th June 1974, before it had even flown. (The plant is now called the 'Sokol' (Falcon) Nizhniy Novgorod Aircraft Factory.) The production version received a new service designation, **MiG-31**.

The first prototype at Zhukovskiy during initial flight tests. The side view shows well the vertical tails located well forward on the Ye-155MP. The K-33 missiles are dummies, since '831 Blue' had no radar.

Above: Close-up of the first prototype's main gear units. The forward mainwheel well doors function as airbrakes; note the skewed rotation axis and the curved shape.

Above: An air-to-air of '831 Blue' during flight tests. Note the larger tactical code and the photo calibration markings on the air intake trunk.

Right: The rear end of the first prototype, showing the wool tufts on the rear fuselage and brake parachute container to visualise the airflow.

Right: '832 Blue', the second prototype Ye-155MP, at the GosNIIAS test range in Faustovo where it was used for ground tests upon retirement; unfortunately no photos of this aircraft in its better days have surfaced yet. Note the photo calibration markings and the small star (a mission marker) on the air intake trunk.

In 1976 Gleb Ye. Lozino-Lozinskiy left the Mikoyan OKB to become Chief Designer of NPO **Mol**niya (Lightning), an enterprise specialising in space systems design, and Konstantin K. Vasil'chenko became the MiG-31's new project chief. In that same year plant No.21 started tooling up for MiG-31 production and the factory's own design office headed by Chief Designer Yevgeniy I. Mindrov was organised in order to support it. The manufacturing drawings were progressively issued to plant No. 21 in parallel with prototype construction (and were revised as the flight tests progressed). Known at the factory as *izdeliye* **01**, the production version differed slightly from the prototypes. The TE flap span was increased, while the area of the all-movable tailplanes (stabilators) was marginally reduced, as were the stabilator travel limits. The vertical tail arm was increased by moving the fin/rudder assemblies aft, the main gear door/airbrake design was altered and so on.

Wearing the tactical code '011 Blue' derived from the fuselage number (line number) 0101-01 – that is, *izdeliye* 01, Batch 01, 01st machine in the batch, the first production MiG-31 was rolled out at Gor'kiy-Sormovo airfield in the late spring of 1977, making its first flight on 13th July. Like the first prototype, it had no radar, being used for stability/handling, fatigue and dynamic strength tests. The fully-equipped second aircraft ('012 Blue', f/n 0101-02), which first flew on 30th June 1977, was intended for checking the capabilities of the aerial intercept weapons system as a whole. These two aircraft, as well as the entire Batch 02 ('201 Blue' through '203 Blue') and Batch 03 ('301 Blue' through '305 Blue') from low-rate initial production (LRIP), were earmarked for test and development purposes.

Stage A of the MiG-31's joint state acceptance trials commenced in May 1977 at the GNIKI VVS facility in Akhtoobinsk (Vladimirovka AB), the LRIP aircraft joining the programme one by one as they were released by the factory. Virtually the entire flight test personnel of the Mikoyan OKB took part in the trials of the MiG-31. These were by no means trouble-free. The engines were especially troublesome, requiring constant modifications and improvements. On

one occasion '011 Blue' suffered an uncontained engine failure and Boris A. Orlov barely managed to land the crippled aircraft. As the engine disintegrated the fragments knocked out one of the hydraulic systems and many other equipment items, and Orlov had been extremely lucky to make it back to base.

GNIKI VVS test pilots joined the action in 1977. The testing of the Zaslon WCS was accompanied by more than its fair share of problems due to the need to test the system's performance in a multiple-target environment; among other things, the instrumented test range in Akhtoobinsk had to be re-equipped so that the initial distance between the interceptor and the target in a head-on engagement would exceed 200 km (124 miles). New telemetry pick-up and trajectory measurement systems had to be installed for tracking the flight of the two aircraft as they closed in on each other; care had to be taken to preclude mid-air collisions, since the trials programme included assessment of target tracking at minimum

Top: '011 Blue', the first Gor'kiy-built production MiG-31 (*izdeliye* 01), seen during tests; the white-pained K-33s are again dummies. Note the 'plus-minus-plus' photo calibration markings.

Above: An air-to-air of '202 Blue', another initial-production MiG-31, showing the deployed leading-edge flaps. Note that the style of the photo calibration markings is different again.

Below: This view of '202 Blue' shows the redesigned main gear doors and airbrakes of the production MiG-31; the airbrakes are smaller, flatter and have a horizontal rotation axis.

range, which meant the separation between the target and the interceptor could be as low as 1 km (0.62 miles).

After successful sorties in which multiple targets were destroyed, even seasoned pilots were awed by the new interceptor's capabilities. Nonetheless, it was exactly the operation of the Zaslon WCS and the radar in particular about which the military voiced the greatest complaints. A special team of analysts from GosNII AS and the OKBs responsible for the system's components was set up to assess the results of the trials and assist in debugging the WCS. It deserves mention that a bench testing complex (BTC) was created in Akhtoobinsk in late 1976/early 1977 pursuant to a Council of Ministers directive for supporting the testing and refining of the S-155 weapons system. The BTC was intended for pre-flight and post-flight simulation of the mission profile, flight crew training (primarily as regards using the data presentation/control systems in the cockpits), verifying the built-in data recording equipment of the WCS and maintaining a 'hot reserve' of the system's electronic components. 30% of its operational time was devoted to radar performance testing and 21% to integrated task simulation, while another 17% was spent on exploring the radar's very high frequency radiation. One of the toughest tasks performed on the BTC was the pre-mission simulation of the simultaneous tracking of four targets, with simulated launches of four K-33 missiles guided simultaneously.

On 28th August 1978 a MiG-31 destroyed four remote-controlled target drones in a four-missile salvo. At the end of Stage B a quartet of MiG-31s demonstrated the possibility of group action to repel a hypothetical air raid against Volgograd in southern Russia. Ten radio-controlled target drones 'attacked' the city, spreading out across a swath 100 km (62 miles) wide; all ten were shot down. Stage B also included verifying the navigation suite in extreme northern latitudes.

In October 1978 a US surveillance satellite recorded the successful destruction of a low-flying target drone by the new Soviet interceptor. This fact was dragged into public view, and the Pentagon's press secretary Thomas Ross, who had stated just a month earlier that 'there is no evidence that the Soviets are capable of shooting down cruise missiles or target drones simulating such missiles', had to eat his words.

Stage A was completed in December 1978 and GNIKI VVS issued a so-called preliminary conclusion clearing the Ye-155MP for full-scale production as the MiG-31. Production began in earnest in 1979; that year the factory released the final LRIP aircraft, '305 Blue' (construction number N69700104801, f/n 0103-05) which made its first flight at Gor'kiy-Sormovo on 27th April and was the first MiG-31 to feature the intended K-36DM ejection seats. (**Note:** In MiG-31 *sans suffixe* c/ns, 697 is a code for

aircraft factory No.21 (it was changed to 384 in 1986), 001 means *izdeliye* 01 (an extra zero is added to give a three-digit product code format) and the rest is the 'famous last five' meaning nothing at all; the first two and last three of these digits accrue independently.)

Stage B of the trials began in the spring of 1979, involving the testing of the weapons system as a whole. The State commission appointed for the trials was chaired by Air Marshal Yevgeniy Ya. Savitskiy, the then Commander of the PVO's fighter arm and a fighter pilot of Great Patriotic War fame. Gradually further test pilots – Aleksandr V. Krootov, Anatoliy N. Kvochur, Roman P. Taskayev and others – started flying the MiG-31, which had entered full-scale production by then. Generally the tests went satisfactorily, although all manner of problems kept cropping up. On one occasion fatigue cracks appeared in the fuselage as Krootov pulled 5 Gs in a turn at Mach 2.6 and 15,000 m (49,210 ft). On another test mission aimed at exploring the aircraft's dynamic strength, the nozzle petals of both engines failed when the MiG-31 was cruising in supersonic mode at low altitude. All failures and defects were carefully analysed and corrective measures were taken.

On 20th September 1979 MiG-31 '011 Blue' was lost during a routine test mission when both engines consecutively caught fire shortly after take-off from Vladimirovka AB. Unable to maintain level flight on one engine in the fully fuelled aircraft, pilot Pyotr M. Ostapenko and WSO Leonid S. Popov ran out of altitude before reaching the base and ejected safely at 350 m (1,150 ft) – the minimum possible altitude.

The joint state acceptance trials of the MiG-31 interceptor, the Zaslon WCS and the K-33 AAM were duly completed in December 1980. The missile was included into the inventory as the R-33 (*izdeliye* 410), receiving the NATO codename AA-9 *Amos*. Finally, on 6th May 1981 the Council of Ministers issued a directive officially clearing the new aerial intercept weapons system for service.

Production MiG-31s had a WCS upgraded in accordance with the trials results; it included an MFBU-410 multi-function missile control module (**mno**go-foonktsio**nahl'**nyy blok oopravl**en**iya; the 410 is an allusion to the R-33's product code). The engines also differed considerably from those powering the prototypes, the production version being designated D30F-6S (**sereey**nyy – production, used attributively) or *izdeliye* 48.

The type's service entry was marred by accidents. The engines and the fuel system proved equally troublesome at first. On one occasion MiG-31 '303 Blue' (N69700104209, f/n 0103-03) piloted by Valeriy Ye. Menitskiy suffered a fuel line failure which caused a massive leak; only the D30F-6's relatively low operating temperature in cruise mode prevented a fire. The

Opposite page:

Top and centre: MiG-31 '61 Blue', an operational early-production *izdeliye* 01 wearing three mission markers to denote destroyed target drones and the 'Excellent aircraft' maintenance award badge. These were the first colour pictures of the type to appear in the Soviet press.

Bottom: A MiG-31 carrying a full load of four R-33 radar-homing long-range AAMs and two R-40TD IR-homing medium-range AAMs.

fighter ran out of fuel shortly before landing and the engines quit, Menitskiy managing a safe off-field forced landing. Inspection of the other four Batch 03 aircraft showed that they all shared the same defect in the fuel system. After this, the Mikoyan OKB undertook a redesign of the fuel system; the changes were to be verified on the third production MiG-31, '201 Blue' (f/n 0102-01), a long-serving 'dogship'. However, on 4th April 1984 this aircraft crashed after developing a serious fuel leak which caused the engines to quit on the way back to Zhukovskiy. As hydraulic pressure fell, the MiG-31 lost control and flicked into a spin, killing Mikoyan OKB chief test pilot Aleksandr V. Fedotov and WSO V. S. Zaïtsev who ejected a second too late.

Despite the initial series of accidents, flight safety soon improved and the MiG-31 proved to be a fairly reliable aircraft. Very few engine fires were experienced in the course of trials and in service due to the engines' lower operating temperature as compared to the R15B-300.

As already mentioned, most production MiG-31s were equipped with K-36DM ejection seats which, unlike the KM-1M, had full zero-zero capability. The first aircraft so equipped, '305 Blue', underwent a large-scale dynamic strength test programme to see how the airframe stood up to the operational loads. In so doing structural reinforcements were made, a new brake parachute container and a new fairing between the engine nozzles were fitted; '305 Blue' effectively became the pattern aircraft for mass production. Various improvements were made in the course of production; the most visible change was the new, flatter upper panels of the air intake trunks which were introduced from c/n N69700128706 onwards, replacing the earlier 'humpbacked' version. Jumping ahead of the story, we may say that the initial version of the MiG-31 sans suffixe stayed in production up to and including Batch 81.

One of the MiG-31's weaknesses was its relatively high landing speed. At a landing weight of 26,600 kg (58,640 lb), the approach speed was 285 km/h (177 mph), exceeding 300 km/h (186 mph) if the aircraft carried a lot of fuel and unexpended ordnance.

The aircraft's capabilities as an interceptor were truly unique. The MiG-31 was the world's first production interceptor to have a phased-array radar. The latter was capable of detecting targets at altitudes between 50 and 28,000 m (165-91,860 ft); it had 'look-down/shoot-down' capability over both land and water. The radar could track up to ten targets at a time while guiding missiles to four priority threats within a sector of ±70° in azimuth and +70°/–60° in elevation. The IRST unit allowed targets to be tracked covertly and infra-red homing missiles to be used. Special electronic support measures (ESM) equipment protected the interceptor from enemy ECM.

The principal armament comprised four R-33 long-range AAMs semi-recessed in the fuselage. Other weapons options were two R-40TD medium-range AAMs or four R-60M agile IR-homing short-range AAMs on two wing pylons, plus the built-in cannon as a last resort.

Mission success was ensured by a unique WCS. The MiG-31's avionics suite allowed it to act as an airborne command post or 'mini-AWACS' if need arose. A flight of four MiG-31s could swap information on targets detected within a swath up to 800 km (496 miles) wide. The aircraft in the flight could distribute targets between them or pass target information to the leaders of other interceptor flights; all data exchange proceeded in automatic mode, using secure channels. Three MiG-31s loitering in a designated area could provide full-time 360° coverage. The aircraft was capable of guiding up to three MiG-23P, MiG-25PD, MiG-29 or Su-27 fighters to their targets without revealing their presence by switching on the radars.

The variety of tasks performed by the interceptors was made possible in no small degree by the crew of two. The pilot was responsible for making the decisions, while the navigator/WSO made the preparations for engaging the target. He plotted and corrected the aircraft's course, processed target information, monitored the tactical situation and selected targets in priority order. Using the telescopic control stick and rudder pedals, he could take over control of the aircraft in case of need.

In 1985 Konstantin K. Vasil'chenko was appointed Director of the Flight Research Institute named after Mikhail M. Gromov (LII – **Lyot**no-is**sled**ovatel'skiy insti**toot**). Anatoliy A. Belosvet became the MiG-31's new project chief for several years.

As compared to its predecessor, the MiG-31 was much more fuel-efficient in subsonic cruise; this made the crew feel more comfortable, especially during overwater flights or maximum-range missions. However, the interceptor's range was considered inadequate; operational Foxhounds based on the Kola Peninsula had to shadow NATO reconnaissance and maritime patrol aircraft at up to 1,000 km (620 miles) from their home base in Monchegorsk, but the PVO wanted more. To remedy this, the Mikoyan OKB teamed up with NPP Zvezda to give the MiG-31 in-flight refuelling (IFR) capability, utilising the probe-and-drogue system. The fully retractable L-shaped refuelling probe was located ahead of the cockpit windshield, offset to port. The IFR system underwent lengthy trials on several aircraft, including a pair of modified Foxbats – the MiG-25PDZ and the MiG-25RBVDZ (the DZ suffix denoted doza**prahv**ka – refuelling).

The first Foxhound to feature an IFR probe was an early-production MiG-31 coded '77 Red' (c/n N69700104695, f/n 0103-04); this was actually a dummy installation and fuel transfer was impossible – the

aircraft served for testing the probe actuation mechanism and for 'dry runs' with the tanker. The greater part of the test programme was performed by Mikoyan OKB pilots in Zhukovskiy, followed by further testing in Akhtoobinsk at the hands of GNIKI VVS pilots.

The next development aircraft was MiG-31 '368 Blue' (f/n 0136-08), which had a fully functional IFR probe and a LORAN system. A test programme was held in which both OKB and military test pilots participated. On 30th July 1987 an OKB test crew comprising pilot Roman P. Taskayev and navigator Leonid S. Popov made the first-ever cross-Polar flight in an interceptor, topping off their fuel tanks twice from an

Top: This early-production MiG-31 coded '77 Red' was the first to be fitted with an in-flight refuelling probe.

Above: Close-up of the extended IFR probe on '77 Red'; the probe was a dummy version and fuel transfer was not possible. Note the cine camera on the air intake filming the contact with the tanker's drogue.

Left and above: Seen here at the GNIKI VVS facility in Akhtoobinsk, '368 Blue' was the first MiG-31 to have a functional IFR system – in effect, the prototype of the IFR-capable *izdeliye* 01DZ.

Above and right:
'10 Red', an operational MiG-31 (*izdeliye* 01DZ), seen at Kubinka AB during an air event. Most of the MiG-31s (*izdeliye* 01DZ) wore the Mikoyan OKB badge on the air intake trunks as shown here.

Below: The pilot's cockpit of the MiG-31 (*izdeliye* 01DZ) '10 Red'.

Il'yushin IL-78 *Midas* tanker; the route took them from Monchegorsk (Murmansk Region) to the North Pole and thence to Anadyr' on the Chukotka Peninsula over areas with few navigation aids and no landmarks. The aircraft was airborne for 6 hours 26 minutes, the pilots using the LORAN system to navigate. Another notable flight covering a distance in excess of 8,000 km (4,970 miles) was made in autonomous navigation mode with two fuel top-ups and an elapsed time of 8 hours 40 minutes; two simulated targets were 'intercepted' on that occasion, including one over the North Pole. With IFR capability the duration of the flight was limited only by the crew's physiological limitations.

At the Gor'kiy aircraft factory the IFR-capable version had the product code ***izdeliye* 01DZ**; strangely enough, the service designation did not change at all (the designation 'MiG-31DZ' encountered occasionally is erroneous). Following one more conversion of an operational MiG-31 coded '31 Red' (c/n N38400171519, f/n 0171-04), the new version entered production in 1989, starting with '74 Red' (c/n N38400181345, f/n 0182-01). It remained in production for a year until it was succeeded by the more refined MiG-31B; the production run was small (about 45 aircraft).

Apart from extending the MiG-31's range, the Mikoyan OKB and its partners consistently worked on improving the interceptor's armament. The need to do so was due largely to leaks of sensitive information about the MiG-31. In 1985 one A. Tolkachov, a spy working for one of the Western intelligence agencies, was arrested in Moscow; the investigators found out that he had passed valuable information on the specifications of

The WSO's cockpit of the MiG-31 (*izdeliye* 01DZ). Note the radarscope and the tactical situation displays.

Mikoyan flight test crews in front of the MiG-31B prototype at Akhtoobinsk. Left to right: navigator Leonid S. Popov, test pilot Valeriy Ye. Menitskiy, test pilot Aleksandr Yu. Garnayev, test pilot Sergey P. Khazov and test pilot Pavel N. Vlasov. The vehicle is an APA-80 ground power unit.

'592 Blue', the MiG-31B prototype, banks away from the camera with the IFR probe deployed, showing the additional wing pylons outboard of the standard ones. The aircraft carries two dummy R-40s (note the conical noses similar to the R-40R version, which the MiG-31 does not carry!) and four R-33s.

the MiG-31's avionics and armament to his Western 'employers'. Tolkachov's actions were even more damaging than Viktor Belenko's defection. As a result, the design bureaux had to step up their efforts to equip the production MiG-31 with a new weapons system.

The work went ahead in two directions. Firstly, the Mikoyan OKB and its subcontractors worked on the radically upgraded MiG-31M featuring an all-new weapons system (see below); however, this aircraft would take a lot of time to test and perfect, to say nothing of series production. Hence in 1987 the Mikoyan OKB made an attempt to boost the combat potential of the MiG-31 and eliminate the shortcomings noted after the state acceptance trials. These measures, combined with a number of new features developed by the OKB and the Gor'kiy factory in the 1980s, resulted in a new version designated **MiG-31B** (*izdeliye* 01B). The design effort was headed by E. K. Kostroobskiy.

The principal changes introduced on the MiG-31B were as follows. An upgraded Zaslon-A (S-800A) WCS based on the RP-31A radar with an A-15A mainframe computer was fitted; provision was made for new tactical information exchange and weapons control modes ('downloading' target information to ground command posts or other aircraft – not necessarily sister ships, 'tandem guidance' in which another air-

Opposite page:

MiG-31B '77 Blue' with a representative array of weapons at Savasleyka AB. There are four R-60Ms and cannon ammunition in the front row and four R-33s, with two R-40TDs in between, in the back row. The red noses of the R-33s are protective covers, hence the odd shape.

Head-on view of a MiG-31B as it vacates the runway after a training sortie. Note the empty APU-60-2 paired launch rails for R-60M AAMs on the inboard pylons and the deployed periscope in the WSO's cockpit.

A pair of MiG-31Bs top up their fuel tanks from Il-78M '32 Blue'.

Above: The pilot's cockpit of a MiG-31B.   **Below:** The WSO's cockpit of a MiG-31B.

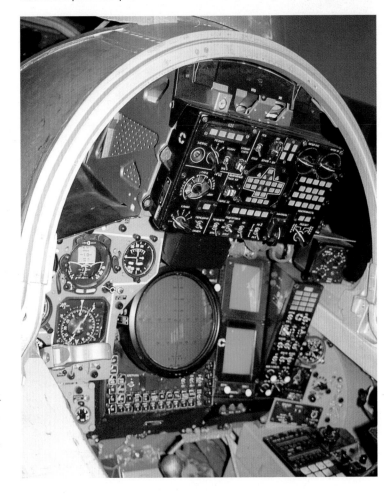

craft's fire control radar is used for guiding the interceptor's missile and the like). The primary armament consisted of improved R-33S AAMs featuring a longer 'kill' range (160 km/99 miles) and active radar homing at the terminal guidance phase instead of SARH; additional IR-homing missiles could be carried on the wing pylons whose number was increased from two to four. Like the MiG-31 (*izdeliye* 01DZ), the MiG-31B featured an IFR system; an upgraded navigation computer compatible with LORAN and satellite navigation systems was installed to enhance navigation accuracy in high latitudes, as were a more capable ECM system and an *Ekran* (Screen) built-in test equipment/crew alerting system (BITE/CAS) replacing the earlier RIU recording/indication device (*reghist**ree**ruyushcheye indit**see**ruyushcheye oo**stroy**stvo*). The flight control system was also updated.

The MiG-31B prototype was apparently coded '592 Blue' (c/n N38400160188, f/n 0159-02). The new version superseded the MiG-31 (*izdeliye* 01DZ), to which it was outwardly all but identical, on the production line in 1990. The product code was soon changed to *izdeliye* 12, MiG-31B c/ns commencing N384012.

At various times such nations as Iran, Syria, Libya and China showed an interest in the MiG-31. Therefore, in the early 1990s a production MiG-31B (c/n N38401208786, f/n 1209-03) was converted into a demonstrator designated **MiG-31E** (*eks*portnyy – export, used attributively), receiving a distinctive blue/white/grey colour scheme and the tactical code '903 White'. The MiG-31E had a somewhat downgraded avionics fit (notably a different IFF transponder and a simplified ECM system) and was armed with four R-33s in an export version and two or four 'dogfight missiles' on the wing pylons. Nevertheless, it was still capable of acting as an airborne command post for other fighter types operated by the nations listed above, such as the MiG-21, MiG-23 and MiG-29; hence even the purchase of a couple of MiG-31Es could bolster the customer nation's air defence appreciably. '903 White' made its public debut at the ILA-92 airshow at Berlin-Schönefeld in June 1992. A little earlier, at the end of May 1992, a Sino-Russ-

A fine shot of the strikingly painted MiG-31E demonstrator, '903 Blue', climbing in full afterburner.

The MiG-31E carrying a full complement of dummy missiles. Note the badge of the 'Sokol' Nizhniy Novgorod Aircraft Factory on the air intake.

ian agreement providing for the delivery of 24 MiG-31s in an IFR-capable version to the Chinese People's Liberation Army Air Force (PLAAF) was signed; the first five interceptors were to be delivered in June 1992. Licence production at the Shenyang Aircraft Industry Company (SAIC) was also envisaged; the first Chinese-built MiG-31 was to be rolled out in late 1994, with production proceeding at a rate of four per month up to the year 2000. However, by the mid-1990s China revised its plans, choosing to buy and build other Russian fighters – the single-seat

Su-27SK *Flanker-B* and the two-seat Su-30MKK *Flanker-G* whose main advantages were multi-role capability and super-agility. Thus the MiG-31 was never exported.

The break-up of the Soviet Union and the ensuing political and economic turmoil caused MiG-31 production to be discontinued in 1993 because the Russian Ministry of Defence had no funds to order more. The production run totalled 505 aircraft, more than 300 of which remained on strength with the Russian Air Force at the turn of the century.

Upgrades
and Special Versions

Russian Air Force
MiG-31BS
'82 Blue'/RF-92305
taxies at Savasleyka AB,
showing the unit badge
of the 3958th Aviation
Base. The absence of
the IFR probe is
noteworthy.

oncurrently with the development and production entry of the MiG-31B the Mikoyan OKB – renamed MAPO MiG (*Moskovskoye aviatsionnoye proizvodstvennoye obyedineniye* – Moscow Aircraft Production Association) in the 1990s – and the PVO launched a mid-life update (MLU) programme to upgrade operational MiG-31s *sans suffixe* to MiG-31B standard. The upgrade work was performed by the manufacturer (by then known as the 'Sokol' Nizhniy Novgorod aircraft factory). By analogy with the MiG-25PDS, which was a MiG-25P updated to MiG-25PD standard, such aircraft were designated **MiG-31BS (*izdeliye* 01BS)**, the S denoting *stroyevoy* (in this case, operational) to distinguish them from new-build 'Bs. The MiG-31BS had the same avionics/weapons fit as the MiG-31B but lacked the latter version's IFR probe, as installing it would require too extensive changes to the forward fuselage structure. Thus the capabilities of existing MiG-31s were enhanced at minimum cost. Outwardly the MiG-31BS was identical to the original version; you had to look into the cockpits to tell the difference.

When state funding of military programmes was curtailed after the break-up of the Soviet Union and the MiG-31M programme was put on hold, in 1997 RSK MiG launched a further MLU programme for the Russian Air Force MiG-31Bs, upgrading them to a new multi-role version designated

MiG-31BM – the first aircraft thus designated; the M stood for *modernizeerovannyy* (updated). In addition to a much-enhanced counter-air capability thanks to R-77, R-33S and R-37 AAMs, the aircraft was to have a tactical strike capability, carrying air-to-surface missiles (Kh-25, Kh-31, Kh-59, Kh-29) and guided bombs (KAB-500 and KAB-1500), with a total ordnance load of up to 8,000 kg (17,640 lb). The new AAMs were to expand the targets' speed and altitude envelope, enabling the destruction of such targets as theatre and intermediate-range ballistic missiles, hypersonic and transatmospheric vehicles.

The aircraft was to feature an upgraded WCS. In particular, the radar was to be upgraded in order to extend the acquisition range against controlled and ballistic aerial targets to 320 km (198 miles) and 'kill' range to 280 km (174 miles) and enable detection of small surface targets on land and at sea. The upgraded radar was capable of tracking up to 15 targets while guiding missiles to six priority threats. The aircraft was expected to be capable of intercepting targets travelling at speeds up to Mach 6. Overall, the MiG-31BM's combat efficiency in counter-air mode was increased by a factor of 2.6.

The **Roos**skaya *Avionika* (= Russian Avionics) Joint-Stock Co. based in Zhukovskiy developed a completely new layout for the MiG-31BM's cockpits. On the standard *Foxhound* the pilot had no idea

Two more MiG-31BSs from Savasleyka, '85 Blue' and '86 Blue', seen participating in the V-Day parade in Moscow on 9th May 2012. Note the APU-60-2 launchers.

'58 Blue', the first prototype of the original (that is, strike-capable) MiG-31BM. The blue-striped radome has been borrowed from MiG-31 '374 White' which wears a demonstrator colour scheme.

what the WSO was doing until the latter told him, lacking tactical situation awareness. To remedy this, the MiG-31BM had a 6x8" liquid-crystal multi-function display (MFD) on the pilot's instrument panel; the forward cockpit also featured a new head-up display co-developed by NIIP and NPO Fazotron. The WSO's cockpit featured three 6x8" MFDs which could display all manner of information (tactical situation overview, navigation data, radar imagery, a 'bomb's eye view' generated by precision-guided munitions and the like). The avionics architecture included state-of-the-art data processors and a MIL-STD-1553B multiplex databus. Finally, new ECM equipment was fitted.

The first prototype of the strike-capable MiG-31BM was converted from a MiG-31B coded '58 Blue' (c/n N38401214306) in 1998; it was officially unveiled at Zhukovskiy on 12th January 1999 during a presentation for various dignitaries and the media. Seven months later '58 Blue' made its public debut at the MAKS-99 airshow at Zhukovskiy. The second prototype was coded '60 Blue'. Operational MiG-31Bs and MiG-31BSs were to be upgraded to this standard. Still, full-scale tests of the MiG-31BM in this configuration were never performed – for two reasons. Firstly, in late 1999 Mikhail V. Korzhooyev, the then General Director of MAPO MiG, was unexpectedly fired and replaced by Nikolay F. Nikitin. A new broom sweeps clean, and Nikitin immediately axed several programmes launched under Korzhooyev – including the MiG-31BM. A contributing factor was that Roosskaya Avionika JSC was regarded with a jaundiced eye by some of the decision makers because it was a private enterprise. Secondly, because of funding shortages the Russian MoD was more worried about keeping its existing aircraft airworthy; a costly upgrade was out of the question when Russia was still suffering from the 17th August 1998 bank crisis. Thus, the strike-capable *Foxhound* remained a one-off.

The idea of upgrading the *Foxhound* was dusted off in the early 2000s. This time the aircraft, which was again designated **MiG-31BM (*izdeliye* 01BM)**, was a pure interceptor with no secondary strike capability. It had an updated Zaslon-AM WCS featuring an RP-31AM radar developed by the Research Institute of Instrument Engineering named after Viktor V. Tikhomirov (NIIP – *Na**ooch**no-is**sled**ovatel'skiy insti**toot** pri**bor**ostro**yen**iya) and a new *Ba**ghet**-55* (Picture frame) digital mainframe computer replacing the obsolete A-15A. Although the existing B1.01M antenna array was retained, the new mainframe computer endowed the upgraded radar with new operating modes, extending the detection range to 320 km (198 miles); the RP-31AM could track 24 targets at a time while guiding missiles to six priority threats at 280 km (174 miles) range. In addition to the R-33 and R-33S, the MiG-31BM's main weapons included the new R-37M long-range AAM developed for the MiG-31M (see below); pro-

visions were also made for carrying four R-77 medium-range active radar-homing AAMs or four R-73 short-range IR-homing AAMs, and the ordnance load was 3,000 kg (6,610 lb). Changes were also made to the cockpits, which were equipped with colour MFDs; a satellite navigation system was also added. The only external identification feature of the MiG-31BM was a faired rear view mirror on the pilot's canopy.

The MiG-31BM's WCS enabled some exotic weapons application scenarios, such as taking over guidance of a missile launched by another fighter without switching on its own radar. Depending on the specific mission, combat efficiency rose by a factor of 1.5 to 4 as compared to the standard MiG-31B; this is an important factor in restoring Russian air power in Siberia and the Far East where Air Force units had suffered considerable cutbacks in the 1990s.

The maximum take-off weight rose slightly to 46,835 kg (103,250 lb); flight performance was virtually unchanged, with a maximum speed of 3,000 km/h (1,863 mph), a cruising speed of 2,500 km/h (1,552 mph) and a marginally lower service ceiling of 20,000 m (65,620 ft). Range in subsonic mode with four missiles was 2,400 km (1,490 miles) on internal fuel only or 3,000 km (1,863 miles) with drop tanks, providing the missiles were launched halfway through the mission; endurance was 2 hours 35 minutes and 3 hours 38 minutes

An inert Kh-31P anti-radar missile (inboard) and a dummy R-77 AAM under the port wing of the MiG-31BM prototype.

The starboard wing of the MiG-31BM prototype, with an inert Kh-58 anti-radar missile and a dummy R-77. Note the nose-up attitude of the R-33 missiles under the fuselage.

Right: The pilot's cockpit of MiG-31BM '58 Blue', note the single liquid-crystal MFD on the right-hand side of the main instrument panel and a smaller second display on the starboard console.

Below: The WSO's cockpit of the same aircraft, with three MFDs on the main instrument panel and a smaller second display on the starboard console. The data presentation system was supplied by the Roosskaya Avionika JSC.

Opposite page, top: The second prototype MiG-31BM, '60 Blue', at Akhtoobinsk. This aircraft and '58 Blue' were further modified as the prototypes of the current (pure interceptor) MiG-31BM.

respectively. Range in supersonic mode with four missiles launched halfway through the mission was 1,300 km (807 miles), with an endurance of 44.4 minutes.

The prototypes were converted from the two original MiG-31BMs, '58 Blue' and '60 Blue'. Later, two more aircraft were upgraded by the 'Sokol' Nizhniy Novgorod Aircraft Factory and delivered to the Russian Air Force's 4th State Aircrew Conversion & Hardware Evaluation Centre at Lipetsk-2 AB for evaluation in late March 2008; the actual testing took place at the Centre's Savasleyka branch (the former 148th TsBP i PLS). Stage A of the joint state acceptance trials was completed that year, and the trials were successfully concluded in 2012. A little earlier, in 2011, the Russian Ministry of Defence contracted the United Aircraft Corporation (UAC), a Russian aircraft industry conglomerate, to upgrade 60-plus MiG-31 to MiG-31BM standard by 2020 as part of the State Arms Purchase Programme for 2011-2020. The job was again performed by the 'Sokol' plant, which is part of the UAC; the first 15 refurbished and upgraded *Foxhounds* were redelivered to the Russian Air Force in 2012.

When all of the Russian Air Force's MiG-31Bs had been upgraded to MiG-31BM standard, the PVO turned its attention to the MiG-31BSs. Aircraft with sufficient service life remaining are being updated to the same standard as regards the avionics but do not have the IFR system; such aircraft are designated **MiG-31BSM** (*izdeliye* 01BSM) and are outwardly identifiable by the rear view mirror on the pilot's canopy, just like on the MiG-31BM. Two MiG-31BSM prototypes – '24 Red'/RF-95437 and '25 Red' – were delivered to the 929th GLITs in early 2014 to undergo state acceptance trials, and others are being modified by the Sokol factory (for example, '07 Blue'/RF-95439). Many of these aircraft have been taken out of storage at Lipetsk where they had been consigned during the Russian Air Force's lean years.

In the mid-1980s, when anti-missile defence (AMD) programmes were strongly on

Left: MiG-31B '592 Blue' was likewise modified under the MiG-31BM programme; note the new wing pylons for carrying R-73 IR-homing AAMs.

Below: MiG-31BM '93 Blue' retracts its landing gear as it departs Savasleyka AB on a training sortie. This was one of the first operational *Foxhounds* to be upgraded to MiG-31BM standard.

the agenda, the Mikoyan OKB brought out a highly specialised version of the MiG-31 – a suborbital launch vehicle for an anti-satellite ballistic missile. This was the Soviet counterpart of the US system based on the McDonnell Douglas F-15 Eagle fighter and the ASAT missile; the latter was known as a suborbital ballistic kinetic kill vehicle (SBKKV), since it did not have an explosive charge and was supposed to destroy the target with a direct hit. In contrast, the Soviet anti-satellite missile, which had been under development at MKB Vympel since 1978, was to feature a conventional (that is, non-nuclear) explosive warhead.

The aircraft was designated **MiG-31D**; the in-house product code was *izdeliye* 07, hence the two prototypes built by the Gor'kiy factory in 1986 and 1987 were coded '071 Blue' and '072 Blue'. Due to the programme's top secret nature the MiG-31D was referred to as a 'weather reconnaissance aircraft' at the OKB in order to fool potential spies!

The aircraft differed from the basic MiG-31 (*izdeliye* 01) primarily in lacking the latter's armament and WCS. Instead, the MiG-31D featured mission avionics enabling it to follow the complex flight path required to set the missile's INS for launch. There was no radar, the nose housing 200 kg (440 lb) of ballast; hence the dielectric radome was substituted with a metal nosecone. The recesses in the fuselage underside for the R-33 missiles were eliminated; the single large *izdeliye* 79M6 missile (eloquently codenamed *Kontakt*) was carried on a special centreline pylon which lowered it clear of the fuselage before launch. Development of the MiG-31D's specialised weapons system at the Mikoyan OKB was supervised by V. M. Polyakov. The LERXes were enlarged, featuring the same curved shape as on the MiG-31M. To ensure directional stability with the missile in place, large delta-shaped endplate fins similar to those of the Ye-155P-5 interceptor prototype were fitted to the wings.

During the mission the aircraft was to accelerate in level flight and then pull up into a zoom climb, maintaining the correct altitude, speed, trajectory angle and geographic co-ordinates, and follow a pre-planned time schedule before launching the missile. The avionics enabled automatic course correction using commands from the ground control centre.

According to the project the MiG-31D was a single-seater – there was no need for a WSO, since the launch sequence was largely automated. However, this had to be changed when it came to the flight tests. In 1987 Merited Test Pilot Aviard G. Fastovets flew the MiG-31D on its maiden flight ('072 Blue' was the first to fly). This was the last aircraft which he tested; failing health forced Fastovets to quit flying in 1990. In fact, as early as 1987 the medical examiners had banned him from flying any aircraft which did not have dual controls (so that another pilot would be there to take over, should Fastovets feel unwell). However, Mikoyan OKB

chief test pilot Valeriy Ye. Menitskiy was firm in his belief that only a top-notch pilot like Fastovets could take the machine (which was expected to be quite a handful) up on its first flight. Hence the prototype had to be fitted with a second set of controls in order to comply with the medics' requirements and the rear cockpit was retained.

The two prototypes underwent tests for several years; in addition to Fastovets, the MiG-31D was flown by Anatoliy N. Kvochur and Toktar O. Aubakirov, and the greater part of the programme was performed on '072 Blue'. In 1987-1992 the MiG-31D made more than 100 test launches of the missile at

Opposite page:
The pilot's cockpit of an operational MiG-31BM, showing the different MFD which has a square shape and is placed higher.

The WSO's cockpit of the same aircraft, with two large MFDs offset to starboard.

This page:
'25 Red', one of the two prototypes of the MiG-31BSM – an upgrade of the MiG-31BS – at Akhtoobinsk. This view shows that the MiG-31BSM has the MiG-31BM's characteristic rear view mirror on the front cockpit canopy but lacks IFR capability. Note the badge of the 929th GLITs and the unusual placement of the tactical code on the air intake.

'24 Red'/RF-95437, the other MiG-31BSM prototype, on final approach to Akhtoobinsk. When seen from the starboard side, the MiG-31BSM is indistinguishable from the MiG-31BM.

'072 Blue', the second of the two MiG-31D 'satellite killer' aircraft, rotates on take-off at Zhukovskiy in the late 1980s. Note the phot calibration markings and the MiG badge on the air intake.

The same aircraft on short finals to Zhukovskiy after a test flight. Note the distinctive delta-shaped wing endplates increasing directional stability with the anti-satellite missile attached.

MiG-31D '072 Blue' hangared at Sary-Shagan AB in Kazakhstan. The *izdeliye* 79M6 anti-satellite missile on its ground handling dolly can be seen on the left; note the folding cruciform stabilisers. The extreme nose is painted dark grey to represent a normal radome, but the visible skin joint lines reveal that it is an all-metal fairing.

A model of the proposed MiG-31I launch platform with the Ishim space launch vehicle (SLV) suspended; note the fairing enclosing the SLV's front end and the differently shaped wing endplates. The size of the rocket would obviously necessitate a much taller landing gear.

the Sary-Shagan missile test range in Kazakhstan and was deemed ready for service introduction. However, in 1992 the programme was put on ice due to lack of funding, at least one (or both) of the MiG-31Ds remaining at Sary-Shagan AB (aka Priozyorsk, the Russian name meaning 'lakeside town' as a reference to Lake Balkhash).

In 1997 MAPO MiG started work on a suborbital launch system based on the MiG-31D. Designated **MiG-31S** (*spetsiahl'nyy* – special), it was intended for placing small satellites into low Earth orbit; in this case the requirements concerning the launch co-ordinates and the setting accuracy of the rocket's INS were much less stringent. The aircraft was to carry the RN-S ballistic rocket (*raketa-nositel', samolyotnaya* – aircraft-launched space launch vehicle) developed by GMKB Vympel; the payload placed into orbit ranged from 40 to 200 kg (88-440 lb). The launch was to take place at an altitude of 17,000 m (55,770 ft) with the aircraft flying at 3,000 km/h (1,863 mph). The first test launch was planned for 1999 or 2000; still, the MiG-31S was never built.

In 2004 the concept was briefly revived when RSK MiG (*Rosseeyskaya samolyotostroitel'naya korporahtsiya* – Russian Aircraft Corporation, as the company was known by then) teamed up with the Kazakhstan Space Agency (Kazkosmos) to launch the *Ishim* programme (named after a city in the Tyumen' Region of Russia). A Russian-Kazakh inter-government agreement to this effect was signed in November 2005. The Ishim suborbital launch system was intended for placing numerous small satellites into various orbits at short notice, and the MiG-31D was regarded as the most suitable launch platform. Apart from the suitably modified MiG-31Ds, which were redesignated **MiG-31I** (the suffix denoting Ishim), it comprised a three-stage SLV of 0.94 m (3 ft 1 in) diameter and an airborne measuring and control station based on the Il'yushin Il-76MD *Candid-B* military transport (almost certainly the 'aircraft 976' *Mainstay-C* used by LII for supporting test launches of ballistic and cruise missiles since the late 1980s). The solid-propellant SLV was designed by the Moscow Institute of Thermal Technology (MIT – *Moskovskiy institoot teplotekhniki*); this odd-sounding name was meant to disguise the establishment's specialisation, which was the development of ballistic missiles.

A model of the MiG-31I showed that the SLV was attached to the aircraft via a large fairing, which suggested that the aircraft was to have a redesigned and much taller landing gear to ensure adequate ground clearance. With the SLV attached, the MiG-31I was to have a take-off weight of 50,000 kg (110,230 lb). The launch would take place up to 600 km (372 miles) from the base with the aircraft flying at 15,000-18,000 m (49,210-59,060 ft) and 2,120-2,230 km/h (1,316-1,385 mph). The payload placed into orbit would be up to 160 kg (352 lb) for an orbit 300 km (186 miles) high or 120 kg (265 lb) for

an orbit 600 km (372 miles) high, and the orbit's parameters (type, inclination and so on) could vary widely. Kazkosmos envisaged using the Sary-Shagan range for the launches; alternatively, the MiG-31I could operate from the territory of the nation commissioning the launch.

In 2005 the Russian Air Force's 929th State Flight Test Centre named after Valeriy P. Chkalov (GLITs – *Gosudarstvennyy lyotno-ispytahtel'nyy tsentr*, formerly GNIKI VVS) undertook research within the Ishim programme. In 2006 Kazkosmos presented the programme at the Asian Aerospace 2006 airshow in Singapore. Shortly afterwards, however, Kazakhstan pulled out of the project, denouncing it as not economically viable; Kazkosmos chairman Talgat A. Musabayev, a former Soviet cosmonaut, stated that it was impossible to find a market for the Ishim system. He was supported by the Kazakh MoD's Chief of General Staff Army Gen. Mukhtar K. Altynbayev, who said that adapting the MiG-31D for the Ishim system would require major changes and the required investments might be inexpedient.

One more project of a suborbital launch system based on the MiG-31 and designated *Mikron* (Micron) was developed by the Astra Research Centre, a subdivision of the Moscow Aviation Institute (MAI). Regrettably no details are known.

TMKB *Soyooz* (*Toorayevskoye mashinostroitel'noye konstrooktorskoye byuro* – 'Union' Toorayevo Machinery Design Bureau), an engine design bureau based in the Toorayevo industrial area of Lytkarino town (Moscow Region), is considering using the MiG-31 as the launch platform for its hypersonic flying testbed intended for testing scramjet engines. The testbed, which resembles a heavy rocket projectile from an army multiple launcher rocket system (MLRS), is to be carried on the centreline; apparently this will not require major changes to the aircraft.

The most improbable project involving the MiG-31 is a passenger transport system called **MiGBus** (by analogy with 'airbus' perhaps?). It involves carrying a small aerial vehicle piggy-back in similar manner to the Lockheed YF-12/D-50 drone combination and launching it in flight. The vehicle, which has a cigar-shaped fuselage, low-set unswept trapezoidal wings of low aspect ratio (not unlike those of the Lockheed F-104 Starfighter) and conventional swept tail surfaces, seats 12 persons two-abreast under an almost full-length canopy which is flush with the top of the fuselage. The artist's impression does not show any air intakes or nozzle; for that matter, the space in the rear fuselage not occupied by the cabin seems too small even for a rocket motor. The biggest question, however, is *who is the system intended for?*

The prototypes and production *Foxhounds* participated in a multitude of research and development programmes involving interception of targets flying at ultra-low level, exploration of radar returns from the ground, guidance using satellites

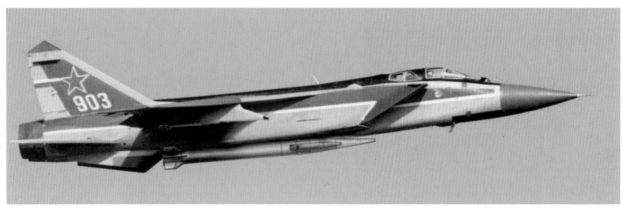

This page:
An artist's impression of a MiG-31 carrying the hypersonic flying testbed developed by TMKB Soyooz.

An artist's impression of the MiGBus. There seems to be very little room for a powerplant in the passenger aerial vehicle's rear end.

Opposite page:
The MiG-31LL-SAPS ejection seat testbed ('79 Red') pared in front of a jet blast deflector at Akhtoobinsk, with the rear canopy in place.

The MiG-31LL-SAPS makes a low-level pass with the airbrakes deployed during an 'open house' at Akhtoobinsk; note the wingtip camera pods.

The same aircraft is seen on landing; the rear canopy has been detached and the soot stains aft of the cockpit reveal that an ejection has been performed for demonstration purposes.

and over-the-horizon (OTH) targeting radars and so on. They were also used for testing new hardware. For example, MiG-31 '79 Red' (c/n N69700116548) belonging to GNIKI VVS (later the 929th GLITs) was modified for testing ejection seats and training flight crews in ejection procedures. This aircraft was designated **MiG-31LL-SAPS** (*letayushchaya laboratoriya [dlya ispytahniya] sistemy avareeynovo pokidahniya samolyota* – ejection system testbed); the Russian term *letayushchaya laboratoriya* (lit. 'flying laboratory') is used indiscriminately for all sorts of testbeds and research/survey aircraft. Outwardly the testbed differed from standard MiG-31s in lacking the glazing on the fixed canopy section between the two hinged portions and having cigar-shaped camera pods at the wingtips to record the ejection sequence. On 11th-16th August 1992 the MiG-31LL-SAPS was displayed statically at the MosAeroShow-92 in Zhukovskiy with a standard canopy over the rear cockpit; for test ejections the rear canopy section was removed. Curiously, the aircraft sported nose art in the shape of a bald lion's head – a jocular reference to the aircraft's testbed role: the Russian for 'bald lion' is **lysyy lev**, which abbreviates as LL for *letayushchaya laboratoriya*. In September 1995 the aircraft had another show performance, demonstrating the ejection of a seat with a dummy during the take-off run at an 'open house' at Akhtoobinsk on the occasion of the test centre's 75th anniversary. In 2010 the MiG-31LL-SAPS was written off as time-expired and relegated to a target range as a ground target in 2011.

A further MiG-31 coded '97 Red' was used by LII for verifying the landing approach technique developed for the Soviet Union's ill-fated *Buran* (Blizzard) space shuttle. The technique involved a very steep approach followed by a flareout at extremely low level.

In 1995 MAPO MiG unveiled a projected version of the MiG-31 at the 41st Paris Air Show. Designated **MiG-31F** (*frontovoy* – in this context, tactical), the aircraft was to have new avionics enabling it to use most of the air-to-surface missile types on the Russian Air Force inventory. The principal armament consisted of Kh-31P and Kh-25MP anti-radar missiles for the suppression of enemy air defences (SEAD, or 'Wild Weasel') role, or active radar homing Kh-31A anti-shipping missiles. Tactical strike weapons included two Kh-59M or three Kh-59 *sans suffixe* TV-guided air-to-surface missiles; three of the lighter laser-guided Kh-29L or TV-guided Kh-29T ASMs could also be carried. Alternative ordnance loads included three 1,500-kg (3,310-lb) laser-guided KAB-1500L or TV-guided KAB-1500TK 'smart bombs' or eight 500-kg (1,102-lb) KAB-500Kr guided bombs. The laser designator or TV guidance equipment was to be carried in podded form. The maximum ordnance load was 9,000 kg (19,840 lb). In the counter-air role The MiG-31F would carry long-, medium- and short-range AAMs (R-37, R-77 and R-73 respectively); a mixed warload for attacking both ground and aerial targets, such as four Kh-31P/As under the fuselage and four R-77s on the wing pylons, was also envisaged. The airframe and powerplant were to be virtually identical to those of the production interceptor. The maximum take-off weight was 50,000 kg (110,230 lb). Range on internal fuel in subsonic cruise was estimated at 2,500 km (1,550 miles), increasing to 3,000 km (1,860 miles) with drop tanks, or 1,200 km (745 miles) in supersonic mode. Speed performance was expected to be similar to that of the standard aircraft, with a 3,000-km/h top speed at high altitude and a supersonic cruising speed of 2,500 km/h. An export version designated **MiG-31FE** was also envisaged and western avionics could be integrated at the customer's request. The MiG-31F/FE remained a paper project, but it may be regarded as the immediate precursor of the MiG-31BM.

The New Generation of *Foxhounds*

Building on the experience gained with the MiG-25, in the late 1970s the Gor'kiy aircraft factory's Chief Designer Yevgeniy I. Mindrov drew up a list of measures aimed at cutting the MiG-31's structural weight, reducing the manufacturing labour intensity, increasing the internal fuel capacity and improving manufacturing and maintenance efficiency. In so doing he enlisted the support of the plant's Director A. N. Gherashchenko and Mikoyan OKB General Designer Rostislav A. Belyakov. In June 1978 MiG-31 c/n N69700107607 (f/n 0105-03) was earmarked for conversion; the Ministry of Aircraft Industry and the military also endorsed a joint document titled 'Schedule of measures to improve manufacturing and maintenance efficiency, increase reliability, extend the service life and reduce the structural weight of *izdeliye* 01'.

The design documents for the conversion were completed in 1980, and the job was done by the factory's prototype construction shop. Coded '503 Blue', the aircraft was rather different from stock MiG-31s. It featured a wraparound frameless windshield, modified air intake trunks, increased internal fuel tankage, a new brake parachute housing, additional centreline hardpoints increasing the number of semi-recessed missiles to six and so on. It was not until 29th December 1983 that Mikoyan CTP Aleksandr V. Fedotov made the aircraft's maiden flight from Gor'kiy-Sormovo. Yet the OKB's head office in Moscow decided that

the conversion offered no major advantages over the standard MiG-31; besides, '503 Blue' suffered from several apparently insurmountable problems, including a disadvantageous CG position. Thus, while many of the new features did find their way into production, no more aircraft were built to this standard.

However, this was not the end of the story. Development of the much-improved **MiG-31M** (*modernizeerovannyy* – updated) began in 1983 pursuant to a joint Communist Party Central Committee/Council of Ministers directive requiring the Mikoyan OKB to develop an aerial intercept weapons system featuring new ultra-long-range AAMs (then under development at MKB Vympel) and new medium-range AAMs. In addition to packing a greater punch, the aircraft was to feature a more advanced avionics suite.

Known in house as *izdeliye* 05, the MiG-31M was intended for BVR combat at extreme ranges and for controlling a large group of earlier-model interceptors. It differed from the MiG-31B in several respects. Firstly, it had a much more capable Zaslon-M WCS built around a new RP-31M phased-array radar. Target acquisition range was increased to 360 km (223 miles) and 'kill' range to 200-230 km (124-142 miles); the number of targets tracked simultaneously rose to 24, including six priority threats. The MiG-31M also featured an optoelectronic targeting system comprising a new Model 42P IRST and a laser rangefinder.

'051 Blue', the 'hybrid' first prototype of the MiG-31M, languishes at Zhukovskiy with the radome removed and a cover closing the hole where the radar array should have been. The small wing LERXes typical of the standard *Foxhound* and the missing fin fillets are clearly visible.

Secondly, the armament was completely new. The MiG-31M's main weapons were six R-37 ultra-long range AAMs. The new missile created by MKB Vympel was not only markedly superior to the R-33 in performance, having a range of up to 300 km (186 miles), but also utilised a completely different control system – it was statically unstable, which improved agility. The R-37 had a launch weight of 450 kg (990 lb) and a 60-kg (130-lb) warhead; active radar homing was used at the terminal guidance phase. The missiles were carried three-abreast on new AKU-610 ejector racks, the forward three being semi-recessed; provisions were made for carrying two R-37s under the wings. Production R-33S missiles could also be carried; in this case the interceptor's performance would be markedly reduced, but

even so it would be higher than the MiG-31B's. In high gross weight configuration the R-37s were augmented by four R-77 (RVV-AE) highly agile medium-range AAMs on the wing pylons; these had a launch weight of 175 kg (385 lb), a maximum 'kill' range of 100 km (62 miles) and a manoeuvring G limit of 12. Since the MiG-31M was intended for BVR engagements only, the designers chose to dispense with the cannon.

Thirdly, the new weapons and WCS led to major structural changes. Thus, the radar array diameter was increased from 1.1 m (3 ft 7⁵⁄₁₆ in) to 1.4 m (4 ft 7⅛ in), necessitating a redesign of the forward fuselage structure and the radome; this, in turn, required the extreme nose to be angled 7° down in order to improve the pilot's field of view. The

The ill-starred second prototype, '052 Blue', seen from a chase plane during a test flight. The redesigned canopy and the fatter spine are evident. Note the undernose fairing which was absent on other MiG-31Ms.

MiG-31M '053 Blue', the third prototype, parked at Akhtoobinsk with dummy R-77 AAMs under the fuselage. Note the curved fin fillets and the absence of the cannon.

Above: MiG-31M '056 Blue' parked at Akhtoobinsk with dummy R-77s under the wings and R-37s under the fuselage. Note the IFR probe on the starboard side and the old shape of the fin fillets.

Opposite page: MiG-31M '057 Blue' was displayed at the MAKS-95 airshow in Zhukovskiy. Four R-77s were suspended, but not the R-37s. The different design of the MiG-31M's nose gear doors is clearly portrayed here.

The pilot's cockpit of MiG-31M '056 Blue'. Note the small round cathode-ray tube display below the head-up display.

The WSO's cockpit of the same aircraft with four large square displays. The joystick on the right is not a control stick – it is associated with the data presentation system/WCS.

canopy was redesigned – the front cockpit again featured a wraparound windshield, which again improved the pilot's field of view; since the WSO's cockpit no longer featured a second set of flight controls, the rear canopy windows were reduced in size and the forward vision periscope was deleted. The fuselage spine aft of the cockpits was much fatter, housing an additional 300 litres (66 Imp gal) of fuel. The wing LERXes were enlarged and reshaped, receiving a curved leading edge; the shape of the vertical tails, including the fin fillets, was also revised.

The maximum take-off weight was increased to 52,000 kg (114,640 lb), so the MiG-31M was powered by uprated D30F-6M engines with larger afterburners delivering 15,500 kgp (34,170 lbst) in full afterburner and 16,330 kgp (36,000 lbst) at combat contingency rating. Many systems and equipment items were designed anew; for example, the IFR probe was relocated from port to starboard. The WSO's workstation featured four new-generation rectangular displays. Satellite navigation equipment was added, as was new ESM/ECM equipment forming an integrated defensive avionics suite, and provision was made for active jammers in cigar-shaped pods at the wingtips. Interestingly, the higher weight caused virtually no deterioration in the anticipated top speed and service ceiling as compared to the 'first-generation' MiG-31.

The PVO command showed a strong interest in the new interceptor whose capabilities exceeded by far all previous versions of the *Foxhound*. Therefore it was decided to build a pre-production batch of MiG-31Ms for use in the trials programme. As construction of the prototypes progressed, it transpired that there was a complete surplus radar; it made sense to install it in an air-

craft for test purposes. Accordingly it was decided to convert the aforementioned MiG-31 '503 Blue', which had had already been extensively modified, into the first prototype of the MiG-31M. The conversion took place in 1984-85. A new forward fuselage was manufactured at MMZ No. 155 in Moscow and mated with the 'beheaded' fuselage of '503 Blue' in Gor'kiy; appropriate changes were made to the fuselage spine. The result was a unique hybrid which, though it superficially resembled a MiG-31M, differed from it in many ways. For instance, the wing LERXes were of the old type (with a straight leading edge), while the fin fillets were virtually non-existent.

The rebuilt aircraft received a new f/n, 0501-01 (that is, *izdeliye* 05, Batch 01, 01st and only aircraft in the batch), and was aptly recoded '051 Blue'. The maiden flight took place on 21st December 1985 with pilot Boris A. Orlov and WSO Leonid S. Popov at the controls. Yet, as mentioned above, this aircraft did not conform to the project configuration. On the definitive MiG-31M the centre fuselage was widened by some 200 mm (7⅞ in) to increase the internal fuel capacity by more than 1,500 litres (330 Imp gal), the rear fuselage was reshaped and incorporated a larger brake parachute housing, the fins were cropped at the roots. The first true MiG-31M manufactured entirely in Gor'kiy to this standard in early 1986 was the static test airframe (f/n 0502-01), which again was the sole aircraft in the batch. It was followed by the second prototype, '052 Blue' (f/n 0503-01), which made its first flight on 27th December 1986 – again with Orlov at the controls. This aircraft conformed to the specs in both structure and equipment; unfortunately it was eventually lost in a crash.

Production proceeded at a rate of one aircraft per year. Five more prototypes followed, to participate in the joining the state acceptance trials in Akhtoobinsk as they were released by the factory. The third and fourth prototypes ('053 Blue' and '054 Blue', f/ns 0503-02 and 0503-03) featured enlarged scimitar-shaped fin root fillets; these reverted to their original shape and size on subsequent aircraft. The fifth, sixth and seventh prototypes – '055 Blue' (f/n 0503-04), '056 Blue' (f/n 0504-01) and '057 Blue' (c/n N72100106137, f/n 0504-02), also incorporated a few other changes made at the customer's request and as a result of the initial trials. In particular, the wings of '057 Blue' were tipped with ECM pods mounting small trapezoidal fins

projecting up and down at the rear to improve directional stability.

Having got off to a good start, the tests of the MiG-31M effectively ground to a halt in the late 1980s/early 1990s when actual weapons trials began. The designers' wish to create an ultra-long-range missile surpassing the American AIM-54 Phoenix in all respects (the R-37) proved the proverb about good intentions. With so many guidance modes incorporated into the seeker head, it proved impossible to ensure adequate reliability while keeping size and weight within the rigid limits imposed by the customer. As a result, after launch the R-37 invariably proved to have a mind of its own, going anywhere except in the direction of the target.

Due to the economic downturn caused by the disintegration of the Soviet Union, the MiG-31M programme was chronically underfunded. The meagre state funding was spread out thinly over a multitude of programmes; the aircraft design bureaux acting as general contractors allocated only a small proportion of what little was available to the subcontractors responsible for the engines, avionics, systems and armament. As a result, so to say, it was the lack of a high-quality filling that prevented the pie from being baked – the MiG-31M and the other Generation 4+ combat aircraft (the Su-27M *Flanker-E*, the MiG-29M *Fulcrum-E* and later the *izdeliye* 1.44 fifth-generation fighter) were unable to complete or even begin their state acceptance trials.

On 13th February 1992 MiG-31M '057 Blue' was demonstrated to the political and military leaders of Russia and some other member nations of the Commonwealth of Independent States (CIS) at Machoolishchi AB near Minsk, Belorussia, along with the other latest Soviet military aircraft. The data placards in front of the aircraft were covered with black cloth to conceal the 'top secret' figures from the journalists accredited at the event; obviously *glasnost'* (the new Soviet policy of openness) still had a long way to go in 1992!

In April 1994 the MiG-31M achieved a 'world's first', destroying a target drone at an unprecedentedly long range of 228 km (141 miles) during live air-to-air weapons trials at Akhtoobinsk. On 22nd-27th August 1995 '057 Blue' was shown to the general public at the MAKS-95 airshow in Zhukovskiy.

Opposite page:
The cockpit canopy of MiG-31M '057 Blue', illustrating the wraparound windshield and the rear canopy windows which are much smaller than those of the MiG-31 *sans suffixe*/MiG-31B.

The tail unit and engine nozzles of MiG-31M '057 Blue'.

The port wingtip ECM pod of MiG-31M '057 Blue'.

Two dummy R-77s under the starboard wing of '056 Blue'.

This page:
Six R-37 AAMs were accommodated three-abreast under the MiG-31M's belly,

Two unfinished MiG-31Ms languishing at Nizhniy Novgorod-Sormovo in 2012.

However, despite the success of the initial tests, the highly effective weapons system comprising the MiG-31M aircraft, the Zaslon-M WCS and the R-37 missile did not enter production because the Russian Ministry of Defence could not afford to order it in the cash-strapped 1990s. '057 Blue' was the last example to fly, although one more MiG-31M (f/n 0504-03) was rolled out in Gor'kiy in July 1992 and three other airframes (f/ns 0504-04, 0504-05 and 0505-01) were in various stages of completion.

The MiG-31M (*izdeliye* 05) served as the basis for two more advanced versions designated **izdeliye 05B** and **izdeliye 05BM**. No information on these aircraft has been released for publication so far.

The MiG-31 in Action

In early 1980 a handful of MiG-31s were delivered to an operational PVO unit for evaluation. Full-scale deliveries began in 1982; the first units to receive the MiG-31 were stationed in the Moscow Air Defence Zone, beyond the Arctic Circle and in the Soviet Far East.

The new interceptor was particularly needed in the latter two areas where the air defence situation had deteriorated considerably in the early 1980s. US Air Force SR-71A reconnaissance aircraft operating from Kadena AB in Japan and RAF Mildenhall in the UK had been intruding into Soviet airspace for quite a while; in the Far East they reconnoitred the militarily sensitive areas of the Kamchatka Peninsula and Sakhalin Island, and in the High North they penetrated as deep as Arkhangel'sk, another area packed with sensitive military installations. The Blackbird's exceptional speed and altitude performance rendered it virtually invulnerable – then-current Soviet SAMs had practically no chances of hitting the high-flying Mach 3 spyplane. Incursions into Soviet airspace by US Navy carrier-borne aircraft also became more frequent. The MiG-23P *Flogger-G* and Su-15TM interceptors forming the backbone of the PVO Aviation in the Far East were no match for the SR-71s; nor could they oppose on equal terms the brand-new McDonnell Douglas F-15C Eagle, Grumman F-14A/D Tomcat and McDonnell Douglas F/A-18 Hornet fighters. Only a high-altitude, high-speed interceptor armed with long-range AAMs could oppose the Blackbird and other modern reconnaissance aircraft at long range.

By the autumn of 1980, when the MiG-31's test programme was basically completed, the first production interceptors were beginning to reach the operational units of the PVO. However, the first units to receive the *Foxhound* were the 54th **Ker**chenckiy GvIAP (*Gvardeyskiy istrebitel'nyy aviatsionnyy polk* – Guards Fighter Regiment), an operational conversion unit of the PVO Aviation's 148th TsBP i PLS (*Tsentr boyevoy podgotovki i pereoochivaniya lyotnovo sostava* – Combat Training & Aircrew Conversion Centre) at Savasleyka AB, Gor'kiy Region, and the 786th IAP stationed at Pravdinsk, also in the vicinity of Gor'kiy. It was in these two units that the new MiG-31-33 aerial intercept weapons system underwent service trials. The 54th Regiment's honorary appellation had been given for the unit's part in liberating the city of Kerch on the Crimea Peninsula in 1944.

In January 1982 the aircrews of the 174th **Pech**engskiy Red Banner IAP stationed in Monchegorsk on the Kola Peninsula started their conversion training; the unit had received this honorary appellation for its part in defending the city of Pechenga (formerly Petsamo, Murmansk Region) during the Great Patriotic War and was named after Boris F. Safonov, a Soviet Navy fighter ace killed in action. The regiment had previously flown the Yak-28P, converting fully to the MiG-31 in 1983. In September 1983 the new MiGs also arrived in the Far East, re-equip-

Two 764th IAP airmen pose with one of the regiment's MiG-31s, '85 Blue', on the military side of Perm'-Bol'shoye Savino airport. The airmen are wearing different helmets (a ZSh-7 'bone dome' helmet on the left and a GSh-5 full-face pressure helmet on the right), indicating this is a rather carelessly arranged propaganda shot.

ping the 365th IAP at Sokol AB near the town of Dolinsk on Sakhalin Island (not to be confused with Sokol airport in Magadan, which is much farther up north). In the PVO's first-line fighter units the MiG-31 supplanted the 1960s-vintage Su-15TM and the Tu-128, which were getting long in the tooth.

Gradually other PVO fighter regiments re-equipped with the MiG-31; by the late 1980s the type was in service with units deployed at nearly 20 airbases and joint civil/military airports. In the European part of the Soviet Union alone there were the 54th GvIAP at Savasleyka AB, the 57th GvIAP at Noril'sk-Alykel' AP (delivered in 1991), the 72nd **Polotskiy** GvIAP at Amderma AP, the Nenets Autonomous District (delivered in 1987), the 83rd IAP in Rostov-on-Don (delivered in 1993), the 153rd IAP at Morshansk (Tambov Region, delivered in 1990), the 174th IAP at Monchegorsk (delivered in

1982-83), the 180th GvIAP at Gromovo AB (Leningrad Region), the 445th IAP at Savvatiya AB (Kotlas, Arkhangel'sk Region), the 518th *Berlinskiy* IAP at Arkhangel'sk-Talagi AP (delivered in 1985), the 611th *Peremyshl'skiy* IAP at Dorokhovo AB (Bezhetsk, Kalinin Region, now Tver' Region), the 786th IAP at Pravdinsk in the western Kaliningrad Region exclave (delivered in 1981-82; later re-equipped with MiG-31Bs) and the 790th IAP at Khotilovo AB (Kalinin Region, now Tver' Region, delivered in 1993-94). In 1993 the 72nd GvIAP and 445th IAP were pooled to form the 458th GvIAP which took up residence at Savvatiya AB.

In the Urals the type saw service with the 764th IAP at Perm'-Bol'shoye Savino AP (MiG-31Bs/BSs delivered in 1993-94). Siberian units equipped with the MiG-31 were the 64th IAP at Omsk-Severnyy AP (seven delivered in 1987, a further 12 before 1990), the

MiG-31 *sans suffixe* '70 Red' flies over the Russian countryside, displaying the Mikoyan OKB logo on the nose and the Guards badge on the air intake.

MiG-31 *sans suffixe* '08 Red', a 174th GvIAP aircraft, is named 'Boris Safonov' after a famous Soviet Naval Aviation fighter ace.

The hardstand of the Pacific Fleet's 865th IAP – the only naval; fighter regiment to operate the MiG-31 – at Petropavlovsk-Kamchatskiy/Yelizovo airport.

The crew of a 865th IAP MiG-31 pose for a photo, clad in pressure suits and GSh-5 pressure helmets.

350th IAP in Bratsk (five delivered in 1988 and a further 12 before the end of 1989), the 712th GvIAP at Kansk-Yoozhnyy AB (Krasnoyarsk Region, MiG-31Bs delivered in 1993) and the 763rd IAP at Komsomol'skiy-2 AB near Yugorsk, the Khanty-Mansi Autonomous District (delivered in 1984). In the Far East the MiG-31 was operated by the 365th IAP and 777th IAP at Sokol AB (the latter unit re-equipped in 1987-88), the 530th IAP at Chugooyevka AB (aka Sokolovka AB, Primor'ye Territory; delivered in 1989-90) and the 865th IAP at Petropavlovsk-Kamchatskiy/Yelizovo airport (delivered in 1986-87). The 865th IAP was later transferred to the Pacific Fleet air arm, becoming the only Naval Aviation fighter regiment to fly the *Foxhound*.

In Central Asia the MiG-31 served with two units in Kazakhstan – a regiment at Sary-Shagan AB (probably the 738th IAP, 12 MiG-31Bs were delivered in 1991) and the 356th IAP at Zhana-Semey AB near Semipalatinsk (the first batch was delivered in 1986, later the MiG-31Bs from Sary-Shagan were transferred to this airfield).

The regiments equipped with the new interceptors covered two directions of probable strategic strikes by the *potential adversary* (read: NATO) – the North and Far East. However, their first combat task was counteracting the SR-71. The Blackbirds used a harassment tactic, intruding into Soviet airspace to a depth of several dozen kilometres and challenging the PVO system to retaliate. The very short time spent by these aircraft over Soviet territory made it all but impossible to shoot them down with a SAM; yet, the radar systems of the PVO were switched to combat alert mode, and their operational parameters were comfortably recorded by US ELINT aircraft flying over international waters, safe from attack.

Initially the fielding of the MiG-31-33 intercept system did not have any major

A 865th IAP MiG-31 is readied for a sortie, with one of the surrounding volcanoes as a backdrop.

A friendly wave from the pilot of a Russian Air Force/530th IAP MiG-31, '27 Red', based at Chugooyevka AB. The aircraft is wearing nose art, a killer whale, which was later removed.

impact on the number of flights of NATO aircraft along the Soviet borders, yet the cases of these aircraft coming too close became less frequent. For example, until 1984 the attempts of the 365th IAP flying Su-15TMs (or possibly the 777th IAP, which was likewise based at Sokol AB and also converted to the MiG-31 in the 1980s) to intercept the SR-71 proved futile; with the advent of the MiG-31 they quickly made the Blackbird crews realise it was best to stay away from the Soviet borders. As an example one can cite an intercept which took place in the Far East on 8th March 1984: a pair of MiG-31s blocked an SR-71 so effectively over international waters that it had to return to Kadena AB without completing its objective.

As mentioned earlier, the first evidence about the 'MiG-25MP' had reached the West as early as 1976 after Viktor Belenko's defection. Reliable information about the new

MiG-31 *sans suffixe* '31 Blue' sits parked in front of a hardened aircraft shelter (HAS) at a Far Eastern airbase.

MiG-31 (*izdeliye* 01DZ) '11 Red' is caught by the camera a few moments before landing. Note that the taxi light is on, not the twin landing lights.

interceptor's capabilities was not yet available; therefore, proceeding from the knowledge about its progenitor, the aircraft was tentatively allocated the reporting name *Super Foxbat*, which was changed to *Foxhound* in mid-1982. In 1983 the US Department of Defense published provisional three-view drawings of Soviet aircraft based on surveillance satellite imagery. Of all the images of advanced Soviet combat aircraft that were published in western aviation magazines in the early 1980s, the 'Super Foxbat' drawings proved to be more accurate than the rest. Some publications even surmised that the three-view drawing was based on far better-quality pictures obtained through intelligence agents, not the grainy satellite imagery. US satellites

pinpointed at least two intercepts of aerial targets simulating cruise missiles in the area of Akhtoobinsk. In one case the interceptor, which was flying at an altitude of 6,000 m (19,680 ft) shot down an aerial target at an altitude of some 300 m (980 ft); in the other case the target was flying at an extremely low altitude – just several dozen metres (less than 300 ft). Analysis of this information enabled experts to conclude that the new interceptor was considerably more effective than the MiG-25P; its main mission was determined as destruction of low-flying targets with long-range AAMs.

In the autumn of 1985 NATO had the first close encounter with the MiG-31 when the pilot of a Royal Norwegian Air Force/331st Sqn General Dynamics F-16A

MiG-31B '26 Red' carrying four R-33s and four R-60Ms streams vortices from the wing LERXes.

Eleven 54th GvIAP MiG-31Bs and MiG-31BSs sit under wraps on the flight line at Savasleyka AB. Note the unit badge on the nearest aircraft.

Fighting Falcon photographed the new Soviet interceptor over international waters off the coast of Eastern Finmark province of Norway. The photos were published in all the leading aviation magazines of the world and were accompanied by profuse comments. The USA made no attempt to conceal that it was concerned about the deployment of new Soviet weapon systems that could match the performance of their Western counterparts. US Deputy Secretary of Defence Donald Lehman, who was responsible for command, administration, communications and intelligence, declared that the MiG-31 was superior to any US fighter, including the F-15, and had more capable avionics, including a better GCI guidance, control and communication system, better missiles, greater speed and a longer combat radius.

The intensity of the interceptors' operations peaked at the Far Eastern and northern borders of the USSR. This is illustrated by the statistics of just one PVO regiment based on Kamchatka, which converted to the MiG-31 in the second half of the 1980s; in 1987 the regiment's pilots flew 214 missions to ward off reconnaissance aircraft, and in 1988 there were 825 such missions. Much nuisance was caused by the SR-71s, as well as US Navy Lockheed P-3 Orion anti-submarine warfare aircraft and USAF Boeing RC-135 spyplanes. The area of the Kola Peninsula also constantly received the attention of the NATO's intelligence assets. In 1987 the pilots of the 174th IAP carried out 203 missions to escort away foreign aircraft flying along the Soviet border; this figure included 69 sorties to ward off the SR-71s operating from RAF Mildenhall. In 1988 the intensity of the combat work further increased: there were 436 sorties (86 of them for intercepting the Blackbirds); in 1989 the number of intercept missions fell to 270.

Apart from intercepting real-life targets, the 174th IAP took part in various exercises,

including **Sev**er-87 (North-87), Otra**zhen**iye-88 (in this context, Rebuff-88) and others. In the course of these exercises the possibility of deploying MiG-31s to the ice airfield on Graham Bell Island in the Zemlya Frantsa Iosifa (Franz Josef Land) archipelago – the northernmost airbase not

The crew of MiG-31BS '86 Blue', a 54th GvIAP aircraft, prepare for a sortie.

Here, '86 Blue' becomes airborne from Savasleyka AB.

just in the Soviet Union but anywhere in the world – was tested. Working alongside the aircrews of the 174th IAP were the MiG-31s from the Sakhalin-based 365th IAP and the Amderma-based 72nd GvIAP. The latter received its MiG-31s in December 1986, and on 27th May 1987 one of the regiment's squadrons went on quick-reaction alert duty with the type for the first time. The first combat sortie was flown that same day; a 72nd GvIAP crew comprising pilot Guards Capt. Yu. N. Moiseyev and WSO Guards Capt. O. A. Krasnov intercepted an SR-71 and foiled its reconnaissance mission.

In November 1990 the MiG-31 made its first official appearance outside the Soviet Union when a model of the interceptor was demonstrated at a trade fair in Manila. There were plans to show the real aircraft at the IDEX defence trade fair in Dubai in January 1991, but the outbreak of the First Gulf War caused the event to be postponed until October; hence the MiG-31's international début took place at the 39th Paris Air Show in June 1991. Sporting a special blue/white/grey colour scheme (repeated later on the MiG-31E), MiG-31 '374 White' (c/n N69700121496, f/n 0137-04) was flown to Le Bourget by a Mikoyan OKB crew comprising pilot Valery Menitskiy and navigator Yuriy Yermakov, participating in demonstration flights during the last days of the show. The MiG-31's demonstration flights did not provoke any rapturous comments, but specialists estimated it at its true worth, noting especially its engines, WCS and armament. In Paris, when the interceptor was shown in the static park, the radome was detached, exposing the phased-array antenna of the RP-31 radar which attracted enormous interest. Seeing is believing, they say; yet, even after having seen the B1.01M antenna, some American engineers continued to claim that it was a conventional mechanically-scanned slotted antenna. The most serious criticism voiced by western special-

ists concerned the quality of the welding seams in the fighter's airframe, which were crude by western standards. Yet, the most realistic appraisal of the aircraft was given in the *Airshow Daily* magazine which noted that, while bearing a superficial resemblance to its predecessor, the MiG-31 was a completely different machine capable of destroying any hostile aircraft at any altitude, thanks to its all-aspect target detection systems. It was stated that the MiG-31 could not be compared directly to any other new-generation fighter – it was just a good 'warhorse'.

In October the *Foxhound* was displayed at IDEX '91; on their way back from Dubai a group of Soviet aircraft, including the MiG-31, 'dropped in' at Teheran for a quick demonstration to the Islamic Republic of Iran Air Force. In 1992 the interceptor was demonstrated in Britain at the Farnborough International '92 airshow. The MiG-31 repeatedly took part in various other international airshows, including those in Canada and Germany (ILA).

It would be untrue to say that Soviet pilots treated the MiG-31 with 'great respect'. Unfortunately, there were reasons for that. Knowing that the patrol sorties would be of long duration, the designers had taken measures to reduce the MiG-31's fuel burn. However, these measures did not solve the problem; should one of the engines fail, the other engine began to consume so much fuel that range was drastically reduced. More often than not the loitering flights were performed over water; however, Soviet fighter pilots were not accustomed to lengthy flights over the briny, and they often felt ill at ease during such missions. This is where powerplant reliability played a crucial role.

There were other reasons as well for the initial wary attitude towards the MiG-31. In comparison with its predecessors the *Foxhound* proved to be rather strict in handling and 'disinclined' to forgive piloting errors.

Still, many pilots and senior officers were not overly zealous in studying the intricacies of the new hardware, not deeming it necessary to consult the flight manual. Experienced pilots showed no enthusiasm for re-training, and it was dangerous to fly the 'thirty-one' on the off-chance.

Yet, while some pilots mastered the new machine reluctantly, others were enthusiastic about it. The transition to the new machine proceeded rather smoothly in the 763rd IAP at Komsomol'skiy-2 AB (1984) and in the 350th IAP at Bratsk (1988-89) These were the so-called 'youth regiments' which were staffed to a considerable extent by recent graduates of flying schools who had not yet 'lost the knack for learning'. In addition, strange as it may seem, the successful mastering of the new interceptor by these regiments was facilitated by geography: in the outback areas of the North and the Far East there was little else that might serve as a pastime.

The ground crews, too, were somewhat slow in getting to grips with the new machine. As compared to the relatively compact Su-15TM and MiG-23P operated previously by some of the units, the MiG-31 seemed huge, being similar in size to the MiG-25PD. Only technicians who had worked on the Tu-128 could take exception to this impression: the *Fiddler* was dimensionally twice as big as the *Foxhound*.

MiG-31 operations were not free from accidents (both fatal and non-fatal) and incidents. For example, on 8th August 1988 a 174th IAP MiG-31 flown by pilot Maj. Kudryavtsev and WSO Kravchenko suffered an engine fire while flying a mission over the Barents Sea. The efforts to extinguish the fire were not entirely successful, but the crew displayed exceptional presence of mind and managed a safe landing back at Monchegorsk where the blaze was put out. Kudryavtsev and Kravchenko were awarded the Order of the Combat Red Banner and the order of the Red Star respectively. Sadly, in the summer of 1989 Kudryavtsev was killed in a flying accident while performing practice launches of R-33 AAMs during an exercise.

Russian aeronautical magazines cited an incident that occurred in December 1988, when an unwary technician was sucked into the MiG-31's air intake during an engine run.

On 19th July 1989 a 72nd IAP MiG-31 coded '95 Red' (c/n N38400151519) crashed near Amderma airport during a check-up flight after a biennial scheduled maintenance check. Five seconds after lift-off the master warning system indicated a fire in the port engine. Complying with instructions from the tower, the pilot (deputy squadron commander Guards Capt. Nikolay V. Kravtsov) cancelled the reheat, throttling back the port engine to flight idle as soon as the minimum safe altitude was reached. Two and a half minutes after take-off the warning system indicated a fire in the starboard engine as well. 30 seconds later the pilot shut down the port engine and activated the fire suppression system. However, on one engine running at full military power the heavy aircraft started losing speed. Kravtsov had to engage the afterburner of the starboard engine again, switching it off at 600 km/h (373 mph) and 670 m (2,120 ft); after that the airspeed began to drop again, this time at a much higher rate. Attempts to engage the afterburner again were fruitless. When the speed was down to 340 km/h (211 mph), Kravtsov and WSO Guards Capt. M. A. Gorbunov ejected at an altitude of 520 m (1,705 ft). The cause of the fire was traced to a fuel leak resulting from faulty repairs of the port engine's fuel piping. As the port engine was shut down, the flames were sucked into the starboard engine bay due to air ejection and differential pressure; the fire heated the cables controlling the starboard engine nozzle, causing it to open spontaneously to maximum aperture setting and causing loss of thrust. The pilot failed to realise this and did not make use of the emergency device for closing the nozzle, causing the aircraft to decelerate below minimum control speed.

In fact, most of the MiG-31's problems were associated with the powerplant. The Solov'yov OKB had succeeded in reducing the D30F-6 engine's operating temperature to nearly half the value typical of the MiG-25's R15B-300, yet engine fires did occur. Initially it was the cooling turbines that were at fault. They had caused no problems on the development machines, but in series production the supplier started turning out cooling turbines with defective blades. With the turbine operating at 40,000 rpm, the blades broke off and wreaked havoc in the engine bay. The cause of these fires remained a mystery for a long time: as a rule, all that remained of the crashed aircraft was a big crater. Finally, a MiG-31 caught fire at Sary-Shagan AB when beginning its take-off

A MiG-31 undergoes an engine change in the open with the help of a mobile crane on a Ural-375D chassis. A special spreader bar is used to extract the engine.

run. The flight control officer promptly ordered the pilot to abort the take-off; the aircraft overran the runway and burned out completely, but what little remained of it enabled the investigators to trace the cause of the fire to uncontained failure of the cooling turbine. First, this unit was modified by installing an armour shield to contain the runaway blades in the event of a failure; later a redesigned and more reliable cooling turbine was introduced.

After the introduction of IFR capability on the MiG-31 (*izdeliye* 01DZ) and MiG-31B the interceptor's endurance came to be limited not by the fuel load but rather by crew fatigue which caused the airmen to lose concentration, making it difficult to carry out the mission effectively. Moreover, during such a long flight even the crew's need to relieve themselves could prevent them from fulfilling the task, or even provoke an accident. Nobody had given thought to this and designed urinals for the crew. However, persistent shortages of jet fuel in the 1990s and the resulting low utilisation in the fighter units made it possible to forget about this problem for a while.

After the break-up of the Soviet Union most of the MiG-31s were inherited by Russia. Notwithstanding the fuel shortages, the Russian Air Force MiG-31s duly conducted their combat patrols. For example, in 1994 a Pacific Fleet/865th IAP *Foxhound* flown by pilot Maj. A. N. Pshegoshev and WSO Capt. V. V. Velichko scrambled from Petropavlovsk-Kamchatskiy to prevent an infringement of Russian airspace by a US-registered Cessna 550 Citation II business jet which had strayed off the international airway.

On 16th July 1997 the formerly separate Air Defence Force was merged into the Russian Air Force as part of the military reforms. This reorganisation saw many units disbanded – more often than not to cut costs. The PVO was hard hit by the reform – although, in fairness, some MiG-31 units had vanished even earlier. The disbanded regiments were the 57th GvIAP (1993), 64th IAP (1991), 72nd GvIAP (1993), 174th GvIAP (2001), 180th IAP (2002), 350th IAP (2002), 445th IAP (1998), 518th IAP (1998 or 2002), 763rdIAP (1998) and 777th IAP (1997). Many of their aircraft were mothballed at the 4020th Storage Depot in Lipetsk. The Sokol aircraft plant also agreed to keep a number of surplus MiG-31s in storage at Nizhny Novgorod-Sormovo; this was a logical step from the plant, which hoped for an eventual upgrade of the interceptors for the Russian Air Force.

In the financially troubled 1990s, when the pilots had considerably fewer opportunities to practise their flying skills, lack of proficiency and failure to conduct timely repairs of the hardware resulted in more accidents and incidents. 35 accidents and incidents, including 12 fatal crashes, took place in the course of the MiG-31's squadron service up to the year 2000; according to the accident reports, 19 of them were due to crew error. For example, on 31st May 1995 a MiG-31 crashed near Komsomol'sk-on-Amur in the Russian Far East when an engine fire occurred immediately after take-off; the crew succeeded in steering clear of a residential area before ejecting safely. On 6th September 1995, when a 458th GvIAP MiG-31 was launching R-40TD AAMs during a night practice sortie over the White Sea, the port missile failed to leave the pylon as its rocket motor ignited. The aircraft rolled sharply and flicked into a spin; attempts to recover from the spin proved fruitless. Pilot Guards Lt.-Col. Shvetsov and WSO Guards Lt. (SG) Klodchenko ejected and ended up in the drink, the pilot suffering a spinal injury in so doing; after four hours in a bitterly cold and stormy sea they were rescued by a Soviet cargo ship that had been directed to the scene by an Antonov An-26 *Curl* search and rescue aircraft. In the summer of 1996, when practising a landing after a simulated engine failure, a MiG-31 collided with an obstacle during an attempted go-around; the crew ejected, but one of the airmen lost his life.

On 15th January 1997 a 51st IAP aircraft crashed near the town of Oktyabrskiy, Arkhangel'sk Region, during a routine training flight from Savvatiya AB. The crew (Maj. Vasiliy Strizhel'nikov and Capt. Yuriy Shcherbanyov) was killed; the interceptor had dived from an altitude of more than 11,000 m (36,090 ft) and, according to eyewitness accounts, had disintegrated in mid-air. One more MiG-31 crashed near the town of Borisovskiy (Tver' Region) on 26th September 1997 during a training flight from Khotilovo AB when a fire broke out in the starboard engine. After trying unsuccessfully to extinguish the fire the crew ejected and were picked up by the search-and-rescue service; the burning aircraft fell in a wooded area, causing no collateral damage.

The MiG-31 has taken part in numerous exercises and experiments, in the course of which unique information has been obtained on the possibilities of using over-the-horizon (OTH) targeting radars for guidance over thousands of kilometres from the target, on the interception of anti-shipping missiles flying just a few metres over the sea, and of cruise missiles with a low radar signature, on the influence of ground clutter on the intercept precision, etc. For example, the 174th IAP took part in Exercise **Sever**-87 (North-87) in the course of which four crews carried out their combat mission and then, as mentioned above, landed on an ice airfield on Zemlya Frantsa Iosifa. Four MiG-31s temporarily deployed to this airfield also during Exercise *Otrazheniye-88* (Rebuff-88). In addition, in 1986-88 crews from the Monchegorsk regiment flew escort missions with Tupolev Tu-95MS *Bear-H* strategic missile carriers.

One more tactical exercise with research purposes – Exercise *Voskhod-93* (Sunrise-93) – was conducted by the Russian Air

Opposite page:

'75 Red', an early-production MiG-31B, is part of the flight test fleet at the Russian Air Force's 929th GLITs in Akhtoobinsk.

The same aircraft streams its brake parachutes on landing at Akhtoobinsk.

Four 712th IAP MiG-31Bs on QRA duty at Kansk-Dal'niy AB, with a departing An-26 transport in the background. Note the tactical codes repeated in white on the rudders.

Force between 17th and 21st May 1993; it featured a redeployment of ten Sukhoi Su-24M *Fencer-D* tactical bombers and Su-24MR *Fencer-E* tactical reconnaissance aircraft, four Su-27 fighters, six Tu-95MS bombers and eight MiG-31B interceptors from the European part of Russia to the Far East with four fuel top-ups from 13 Il'yushin Il-78/Il-78M *Midas-A/B* tankers.

From the second half of December 1994 a complement of MiG-31 and Su-27 interceptors ranging from two to six aircraft, together with an Il'yushin/Beriyev A-50 *Mainstay-A* AWACS, carried out combat patrol missions over Chechnya for some time during the First Chechen War (1994-96). This was the only case when the *Foxhound* was involved in an armed conflict – although it did not fire in anger.

With regard to its combat capabilities the MiG-31 aircraft is indeed the best in its class. At present it is the world's only interceptor capable of effectively combating the General Dynamics AGM-109 Tomahawk or Boeing AGM-86 ALCM air-launched cruise missiles. The following information was published in the Russian press. A check-up exercise was conducted at the Sary-Shagan test range: the site simulating a target was known, but the time of arrival of a cruise missile to the target and the direction from which it would come were unknown. To protect the site, four Su-27P fighters were loitering at the baseline altitude of 5,000 m (16,400 ft); a similar mission was also performed by four MiG-31s, of which three machines provided full 360° coverage with overlapping and one machine co-ordinated the actions of the group. The crew of one of the MiG-31s noticed an incoming Tupolev Tu-16K *Badger* missile strike aircraft already some 200 km (124 miles) away. The WSO could clearly see on his display how a second 'blip' detached itself from the 'blip' of the target; it 'vanished' instantly due to the difference in the radar signature of the carrier and the missile. However, the approximate direction was already determined, and some time later, at a distance of 70 km (43 miles), the cruise missile flying at an altitude of about 50 m (164 ft) was detected and destroyed. A similar result was achieved by pilots of the 174th IAP when, forestalling the competing Su-27P, a MiG-31was the first to detect and destroy an R-6 anti-shipping missile that had been launched from a submarine in the Barents Sea and was flying at ultra-low altitude.

These experiments received an additional impetus after the merger of the Air Force and the Air Defence Force in 1997, when the ensuing radical reduction of the unified air arm left part of Russia's territory stripped of fighter and SAM cover – an unsustainable reduction in capability which needed to be offset. The Air Force resumed experiments with long-range flights. On 1st July 1998 pilots of the 4th State Aircrew Conversion & Hardware Evaluation Centre's Savasleyka branch carried out a non-stop flight of unprecedented complexity, covering a distance of 8,500 km (5,283 miles) over the European part of Russia in ten (!) hours. In the course of the flight, combat tasks were practised successively near the southern, northern and western borders of the country. Apart from coping with the technical complexity of a long-duration flight, the exercise was intended to fulfil some other tasks. In modern warfare, especially with modest and even dwindling forces available, victory can only be based on concerted action of various means. It was precisely the joint group actions that were practised in the course of carrying out the tactical mission envisioned by the research flight.

The northern section of the route posed the greatest difficulties in this respect. To intercept the 'adversary' aircraft simulated by one of the pairs a mixed group of nine aircraft was formed, comprising an A-50 AWACS, two MiG-31Bs from the 786th IAP, four Su-30 *Flanker-C* interceptors from Savasleyka and two Il-78 tankers. The A-50 loitered in a designated location, monitoring the situation in a large area, and brought all the aircraft into a single group. The MiG-31s, which had taken off from the airbase in Pravdinsk, were flying in the forward echelon; making use of their unique radar, they located the targets at a distance of up to 200 km (124 miles) and relayed the information to the Su-30 pilots from Savasleyka. The fast and agile Su-30s flying some 60 km (37 miles) behind the MiGs were ready to engage their afterburners and attack the adversary, although the MiGs themselves could destroy many targets simultaneously with their R-33 missiles. The simulated interception was successfully carried out at the latitude of Arkhangel'sk (64°30' N). At the moment of interception the aircraft which posed as the 'adversary' were following a course corresponding to the direction from which bombers armed with cruise missiles might be attacking Moscow from the north. The tactics thus tested can be used at any time over the entire territory of Russia and the adjoining waters.

Once again, successful 'combat experience' with the MiG-31 was obtained in the course of a joint exercise at the Ashuluk PVO test/practice range near Astrakhan' in southern Russia on 31st August/4th September 1998 with the participation of air defence units from Belorussia, Kyrghyzstan, Kazakhstan and Russia. Interestingly, the Kazakhstan Air Force was represented there by three MiG-31 interceptors.

Some other important tasks were practised during exercises held in the Far East in mid-September 1999. Operating in adverse weather, MiG-31B interceptors using long-range AAMs shot down the *Malakhit* (Malachite) target missile launched from the Pacific Fleet's Type 12341 small missile boat RNS *Moroz* (Frost). The main purpose of the exercise was to practice the co-operation of the Air Force's fighter aviation and the Navy. The 1999 exercises, unprecedented in their

Opposite page:

A fine study of a fully armed MiG-31BS, '36 Blue'.

A pair of MiG-31Bs flies in echelon starboard formation during a practice sortie. Neither aircraft carries missiles.

MiG-31 '374 White' owned by the Mikoyan OKB was the first *Foxhound* to be displayed abroad. This shot illustrates well the distinctive colour scheme of this aircraft.

54th GvIAP MiG-31Bs '71 Blue' and '73 Blue' escort A-50M '50 Red' during a flypast in 2008.

The reform of the Russian Air Force in 2009, when air divisions and air regiments were replaced by Aviation Bases and Aviation Groups, saw many units disbanded or pooled, leading to such joint operations. Here, 7000th AvB MiG-31s and Su-27s share the flight line at Khotilovo AB.

'12 Red', a former 174th GvIAP MiG-31 named 'Pavel Klimov', moved to a new home at Khotilovo AB. Note the weathered insignia.

scale for the Russian Armed Forces, became a direct response to what was seen as NATO aggression in Yugoslavia.

In another episode a pair of Tupolev Tu-22MR *Backfire-D* reconnaissance aircraft took off from Vozdvizhenka AB in the Far East and flew a sortie within the inner perimeter of the Sea of Japan at a distance of 100 km (62 miles) from the limits of the international waters, escorted by the MiG-31s. This flight stirred much interest on the part of the Japanese military. The *Backfires* succeeded in spotting 12 additional radar sites that had not been put into action when this area was probed previously by single aircraft.

In fairness, one has to note that the MiG-31's unique capabilities could far from always be used to the full during the service introduction stage. That was the case, for example, when the reason for the rather unsuccessful actions of the Syrian Air Force's MiG-23 *Flogger* fighters in the course of the combat operations over Lebanon in 1982 was investigated. The hasty service introduction of the MiG-23ML *Flogger-G* – a lightweight version of the MiG-23M – did not make it possible to study its combat capabilities thoroughly. Therefore, studies were continued as a matter of extreme urgency under the guidance of Air Marshal Aleksandr N. Yefimov at the 982nd IAP based at Vaziani, Georgia, with the participation of pilots from the Tactical Aviation's 4th TsBP i PLS in Lipetsk and the designers of the Sapfeer-23 fire control radar. The main purpose of the research was to study the radar's capabilities during intercepts over mountainous areas. In the course of the work the flights were transferred to Omsk-Severnyy AP where the 64th IAP was based. In the course of several flight shifts the military investigated the possibility of guiding the MiG-23MLs to their targets by means of commands sent from a MiG-31 acting as a mini-AWACS; for this purpose four MiG-31s, which were passing service tests at the time, temporarily deployed to Omsk. The results of the two fighter types' interaction proved clearly unsatisfactory (later the 64th IAP re-equipped with MiG-31s).

In 2000 the Russian Air Force had approximately 356 MiG-31s (though apparently this figure includes those mothballed in Lipetsk). By 2006 the number of operational MiG-31s had dwindled to a little more than 100 aircraft in service with seven regiments – the 458th IAP at Savvatiya AB (Kotlas), the 530th IAP at Chugooyevka AB, the 712th IAP at Kansk-Dal'niy AB, the 764th IAP at Perm'-Bol'shoye Savino AP, the 790th IAP at Khotilovo AB, the Navy's 865th IAP at Petropavlovsk-Kamchatskiy/Yelizovo AP and the 54th IAP at Savasleyka AB (a training unit), not counting the aircraft in storage.

After the brief war with Georgia in August 2008 which revealed severe deficiencies in the Russian Armed Forces, a new stage of the military reform in Russia was begun. In the Air Force the traditional Soviet-era structure with air regiments, air divisions and air armies was replaced by new units – aviation bases and their constituent aviation groups – and operational commands. The Russian Air Force's MiG-31s came to be operated by the 3958th AvB at Savasleyka AB, the 6980th AvB/2nd AvGr at Perm'-Bol'shoye Savino, the 6980th AvB/3rd AvGr at Kansk-Dal'niy AB, the 6983rd AvB/4th AvGr at Tsentral'naya-Ooglovaya AB near Vladivostok (Primor'ye Territory), the 7000th AvB/3rd AvGr at Monchegorsk and the 7000th AvB/4th AvGr at Khotilovo AB. The Naval Aviation's *Foxhounds* served with the 7060th AvB at Petropavlovsk-Kamchatskiy/Yelizovo; this unit was transferred to the Air Force in 2011 to become the 6983rd AvB/8th AvGr.

In October 2012 it was announced that a detachment of MiG-31s would be deployed full time at Rogachovo AB on the Novaya Zemlya ('New Land') Archipelago in the Arctic Ocean; the aircraft would be sourced from Monchegorsk or Kansk. Their mission would be to provide air cover for the ships of the North Fleet in the event of an armed conflict. Up to 1993 Rogachovo had hosted the Russian Air Force's 641st GvIAP flying Su-27 fighters; the base infrastructure was in good condition and basing the *Foxhounds* there seemed to be no problem. In January 2013, however, the Russian MoD scrapped these plans as 'entirely politically motivated and not approved by the Air Force command' after Minister of Defence Anatoliy E. Serdyukov had been fired and replaced by Sergey K. Shoigu.

The second decade of the 21st century saw the fielding of the upgraded MiG-31BM. Thus, in early December 2012 the first six such aircraft became operational with the Kansk aviation group; by early January 2013 the latter had completely re-equipped with MiG-31BMs. In January 2013 the Perm' aviation group likewise started re-equipping with MiG-31BMs upgraded by the 514th Aircraft Repair Plant in Rzhev (Tver' Region), intending to complete the change by the end of the year. In November 2013 the first two MiG-31BMs became operational at Khotilovo AB; this unit was likewise expected to re-equip completely by the end of 2014.

In keeping with a regulation passed in November 2002, most of the operational MiG-31s have now been placed on the government aircraft register, gaining quasi-civil registrations prefixed RF- to complement the tactical codes. Another fairly recent addition is the individual names on many *Foxhounds*, especially those based in Perm' and Monchegorsk.

The latest accident involving the type was on 4th September 2014 when a main gear strut of a MiG-31 landing at Armavir would not extend. After trying in vain to extend the landing gear until the aircraft ran out of fuel, the crew was forced to eject in a safe area.

The 3958th AvB at Savasleyka AB was one of the first Russian Air Force units to take delivery of upgraded MiG-31BMs. Here the unit's MiG-31BMs are seen on a snowbound ramp, with '95 Blue' being attended by an AKZS-7.5M-131 oxygen charger vehicle on a ZiL-131 chassis.

Here the same aircraft is seen immediately before a night training sortie from Savasleyka (note the lack of missiles).

'92 Blue', another 3958th AvB MiG-31BM, at Savasleyka AB with the IFR probe deployed – apparently as part of the pre-mission checks.

MiG-31BM '92 Blue' leads MiG-31BS '85 Blue', also a 3958th AvB machine, over Moscow's Red Square during the 2012 V-Day parade.

A quartet of MiG-31BMs from two different units is seen practicing for the 2014 V-Day flypast. The red-coded ones are probably from the 6980th AvB/3rd AvGr at Kansk.

MiG-31 '37 Blue' taxying at Petropavlovsk-Kamchatskiy/Yelizovo airport displays the new-style Russian Air Force tricolour star insignia.

Above: The airbase at Monchegorsk also came to host a mixed bag of combat types after 2009 and was one of the first to receive MiG-31BMs. Here, a 7000th AvB/3rd AvGr MiG-31BM '03 Blue' taxies past Su-24MR '05 White' (named 'Leonid Yur'yev').

Right and below: 6980th AvB/2nd AvGr MiG-31s on the flight line at Perm'-Bol'shoye Savino, with APA-5D ground power units on the Ural-4320 chassis in attendance. The fighters wear new-style stars, 'VVS Rossiï' (Russian Air Force) titles and quasi-civil registrations introduced in 2012.

'54 Red', a 7000th AvB/4th AvGr MiG-31B from Khotilovo AB, is seen from the refuelling systems operator's station of an Il-78M shortly before making contact with the tanker.

MiG-31BM '10 Red', a 6980th AvB/3rd AvGr aircraft, kicks up snow spectacularly as it departs Kansk-Dal'niy AB for a live weapons practice sortie. Note the R-73 AAMs on the outer wing pylons.

Three red-coded MiG-31BMs bank over a winter landscape, flying in echelon starboard formation.

One more Russian Air Force MiG-31BM, '02 Blue', still in old-style markings.

The only non-Russian operator of the type after 1991 is Kazakhstan; according to press reports, 43 MiG-31s were taken over by the Kazakh Air Force. Currently it has 29 MiG-31s *sans suffixe* and MiG-31Bs in service with the 610th Aviation Base at Sary-Arka AB near Qaragandy (Karaganda). The Kazakh *Foxhounds* have participated in international exercises held under the auspices of the Commonwealth of Independent States' Collective Security Treaty Organisation (CSTO), such as Exercise **Chis***toye* **neb***o-2012* (Clear Skies-2012). Unfortunately the Kazakh MiG-31s have also had their share of accidents; one aircraft is known to have crashed on 23rd April 2013 due to a hardware malfunction, killing pilot Col. Marat Yedigeyev (WSO Maj. Ruslan Galimzyanov ejected and survived).

What next? In April 2013, speaking at a 'round table' conference on the MiG-31 in the State Duma (the Russian Parliament), the current Russian Air Force Commander-in-Chief Col.-Gen. Viktor N. Bondarev stated that a fleetwide upgrade of Russia's MiG-31s would cost approximately RUR 50 billion (US$ 1,581,557,770 at the then-current exchange rate). He said that the MiG-31 was obsolete, requiring complete replacement of the navigation suite and the weapons system; the associated R&D programme would cost around RUR 25 billion (US$ 790,778,880). Bondarev said this money would better be spent on developing of a 'clean sheet of paper' successor to the *Foxhound* which would be 'two or three times better', as he put it; such an aircraft could be developed by 2020. (Actually, the stated service entry date is overly optimistic; a more reasonable approach is that a possible 'Foxhound II' should be developed within the State arms programme for 2016-2025.) Bondarev also said that simply reinstating MiG-31 production after a 20-year hiatus as suggested by Russia's Vice Prime Minister Dmitriy O. Rogozin was impossible and inexpedient, as it would delay the progress of the aircraft industry. Nevertheless, he made it clear that the Russian Air Force is not giving up on the MiG-31. *'We have a host of problems [associated with the type's operation]. Still, we are operating this aircraft, hanging on to it and fighting for it, and we intend to upgrade it to the standard the Air Force needs'*, he added. According to Bondarev, the Russian Air Force had 122 MiG-31s then, plus a number of surplus examples which were in storage but could be upgraded and returned to service; 44 MiG-31s were due for an upgrade.

Speaking at the same conference, Chairman of the State Duma's Committee on Defence Matters Vladimir P. Komoyedov said that Russia should stop scrapping MiG-31s and invest into upgrading them up to 2020 instead. *'Given a properly done upgrade, the MiG-31 all-weather interceptor will be superior to current indigenous and foreign aircraft in the same class for at least another 10-15 years'*, said he.

The MiG-31 has been preserved at several locations in Russia. For example, the Central Russian Air Force Museum in Monino south of Moscow boasts a development aircraft coded '202 Blue' (c/n N69700102176, f/n 0102-02) and a Batch 4

Lately many Russian Air Force aircraft have gained individual names, some of them being named to honour Soviet pilots of Second World War fame. Here, MiG-31 '11 Blue' from Perm' is named 'Mikhail Grib'.

Kazakhstan Air Force (610th Aviation Base) MiG-31s on the flight line at Sary-Arka AB near Karaganda.

A fully armed Kazakhstan Air Force *Foxhound* displays the national insignia with the soaring eagle and sun. Note the markings on the hardstand showing clearly how the aircraft and the ground support vehicles should be parked.

Kazakhstan Air Force MiG-31BS '24 Red' in flight; note the badge of the 610th Aviation Base on the air intake trunk.

Pilot Col. Vladimir Goorkin and WSO Col. Aleksandr Kozachenko pose with MiG-31 '75 Red' after establishing several world altitude and time-to-height records on 31st July and 1st August 2003.

The official FAI diploma testifying that Vladimir Goorkin and Aleksandr Kozachenko have established a time-to-height record on 1st August 2003, attaining 6,000 m (19,685 ft) in 1 minute 50 seconds.

An atmospheric sunset shot of a MiG-31… but don't perceive it as symbolic: the sun is not setting for the *Foxhound* yet.

MiG-31 *sans suffixe* ('96 Blue', c/n N69700106125) which had previously been an instructional airframe in the now-closed PVO Junior Aviation Specialists' School in Solntsevo on the south-western outskirts of Moscow. A MiG-31 with the symbolic tactical code '31 Blue' is preserved on the territory of the Sokol plant in Nizhniy Novgorod. In 1999 a MiG-31 which had served with the 518th IAP became a gate guard at the entrance to Arkhangel'sk-Talagi airport to honour the pilots flying in the northern latitudes.

It deserves mention that the MiG-31 holds a number of Class C-1L world records (that is, for jet-powered aircraft with a take-off weight of 35,000-45,000 kg/77,160-99,210 lb). On 31st July and 1st August 2003 two Russian Air Force crews – a crew from a PVO unit (pilot Col. Vladimir Goorkin/WSO Col. Aleksandr Kozachenko) and a 929th GLITs crew (pilot Col. Sergey F. Seryogin/WSO Col. Aleksey K. Pestrikov) – flew three sorties from Akhtoobinsk in a MiG-31 with four R-33s and a full ammunition load for the cannon. Despite ambient temperatures in excess of 30°C (86°F), they succeeded in beating 22 world records established earlier on the MiG-25; 19 of the new records were officially recognised by the World Air Sports Federation (FAI – *Fédération Aéronautique Internationale*). In some cases the predecessor's result was bettered by a factor of two or more – for instance, the climb time to 12,000 m (39,370 ft) was reduced by two-thirds; the maximum altitude attained was 21,690 m (71,161 ft) which was more than 5,000 m (16,400 ft) higher than on the MiG-25 with an identical payload. Importantly, the aircraft was a standard one, not specially modified for the record attempts as is often the case. The participants stated that the MiG-31 had the potential to break more than 30 other speed, altitude and time-to-height records with or without a payload; further record attempts were tentatively scheduled for March-April 2004.

The MiG-31 in Detail

The following description applies to the production MiG-31 *sans suffixe*. The MiG-31 is a twin-engined two-seat heavy interceptor. 33% of the airframe is a riveted structure made of aluminium alloys designed for operating temperatures up to 150°C (300°F); components subject to strong kinetic heating at supersonic speeds are made of spot-welded stainless steel (50%) and arc-welded titanium (16%), with other materials accounting for just 1%.

The fuselage is a monocoque stressed-skin structure with a cross-section changing from circular to oval with the longer axis vertical (in the cockpit area) to almost rectangular (near the air intakes) to oval with the longer axis horizontal; maximum cross-section area 5.7 m² (61.3 sq ft). The fuselage is built in three sections; it has 57 frames and webs; the principal load-bearing frames are Nos 1 to 6, 6B, 7, 9, 10, 10A, and 11 through 14. The structure is made of VNS-2, VNS-5, EI-878, SN-3 EI-703, VNL-3 and VL-1 high-strength stainless steel, D19 and VAL-10 aluminium alloys, and OT4-1, VT-20, VT-21L and VT-22 titanium alloys.

The *forward fuselage* (up to frame 4) is made chiefly of riveted aluminium and includes a detachable conical dielectric radome, the cockpits (frames 1-3) and avionics bays (web 1 to frame 1 and frames 3-4). The pressurised tandem cockpits are enclosed by a common four-section canopy with a fixed windshield, a fixed centre portion and individual aft-hinged sections operated by hydraulic rams. The windshield features a 36-mm (1¹³⁄₃₂ in) triplex birdproof windscreen; the windshield sidelights and other glazing panels are made of 10-mm (0²⁵⁄₆₄ in) SO-200 heat-resistant Plexiglas. The rear canopy section incorporates a retractable forward vision periscope that can be deployed at up to 700 km/h (434 mph) IAS, enabling the WSO to fly the aircraft. The cockpits are separated by a sloping bulkhead and a 10-mm panel of AO-120 Plexiglas at frame 2; the rear cockpit terminates in a sloping bulkhead, the bulkheads carrying the ejection seat guide rails. The nosewheel well is located between frames 1A and 3V.

The *centre fuselage* (frames 4-12) is a welded stainless steel structure with ten mainframes (Nos. 4-6, 6B, 7, 9, 10, 10A, 11 and 12) that absorbs the loads from the wings, tail unit (via the aft fuselage) and landing gear, as well as the external aerodynamic loads and the air pressure in the inlet ducts and fuel tanks. It incorporates the fuel tank bays, mainwheel wells, equipment bays, attachment points for the wings, air intakes, engines, fins and missile ejector

The forward fuselage of a MiG-31BS. Note the small dielectric panels aft of the radome.

The open cockpit canopies of the same aircraft. Note the twin actuating rams and the deployed forward vision periscope on t^l WSO's canopy.

The insides of the canopies are faced with insulating blankets. Note the pink sealant around the edges of the transparencies.

racks. The air intakes are stressed-skin structures with sharp lips, the side panels slanting aft; the inboard lips act as boundary layer splitter plates. The inlet ducts start at frame 2, running along the fuselage sides to frame 6; the cross-section changes from rectangular at the front to circular between frames 6 and 7 (at the engine compressor faces). The tapering fuselage spine housing the control runs extends from the cockpit canopy to the brake parachute container.

The *rear fuselage* (frames 12-14) incorporates attachment points for the tail surfaces (frames 13 and 14), as well as for the after-

The port wing of a MiG-31 with a PTB-2500 drop tank attached.

burners; it also accommodates engine accessories. Three equipment bays faced with ATM-3 heat insulation are located in the upper aft fuselage between frames 12-13, 13-14 and 14B-14V. The tailcone consists of a centrebody welded from EI-703 steel and a detachable outer portion.

The cantilever shoulder-mounted wings of trapezoidal planform have 41°02' leading-edge sweep on most of the span and small LERXes swept back 70°30'; aspect ratio 2.93, taper 3.14, incidence 0°, anhedral 5°. The cambered wings utilise thin airfoils with a sharp leading edge (TsAGI P44M at the roots and TsAGI P101M further outboard); thickness-to-chord ratio is 3.7% at the roots, 4.1 % at mid-span and 4.48% at the tips. They are one-piece three-spar structures made of VNS-2 and VNS-5 high-strength stainless steel and OT4-1 and VT-20 titanium attached to the fuselage by six fixtures each; each wing incorporates two integral fuel tanks and two external stores hardpoints, the outer pair being 'wet' (designed for carrying a drop tanks). Each wing has a single boundary layer fence on the upper side. The wings feature four-section leading-edge flaps with 13° deflection, two-section flaps (maximum deflection 30°) and two-section flaperons with a travel limit of ±20°. The flaperons may droop 5°, in which case they are deflected 15° up and 25° down.

The twin *vertical tails* consist of fins (with inset rudders) augmented by ventral strakes. The fins canted outboard 8° have 54° leading-edge sweep. They are riveted two-spar structures made of D19 duralumin, with integral fuel tanks in the torsion boxes, and are identical, except for the detachable leading edge fairings (the port fin leading edge is metal while the starboard one is made of Textolite). The detachable fin tip fairings are made of glassfibre/Textolite composite and enclose antennas. The rudders are carried on three hinges each. The ventral strakes attached to fuselage frames 12-14 are canted outboard 12°; they are likewise of riveted duralumin construction with dielectric forward sections. The low-mounted cantilever *horizontal tail* consists of slab stabilisers (stabilators) with 5°22' leading-edge sweep and 1°25' anhedral; they are of riveted duralumin construction, with titanium skin on the leading edges.

The hydraulically retractable tricycle landing gear comprises a levered-suspension aft-retracting nose unit with twin 660 x 200 mm (25.98 x 7.87 in) KT-176 wheels (equipped with a mud/snow/slush guard) and forward-retracting main units. The latter have twin-wheel bogies with 950 x 300 mm (37.54 x 11.81 in) KT-175 wheels in a staggered-tandem arrangement (front wheel inboard, rear wheel outboard); the bogies rotate nose-up during retraction to lie inverted under the engines' inlet ducts. All units are equipped with oleo-pneumatic shock absorbers and all wheels are fitted with brakes. The nosewheel well is closed by a forward door segment linked to the oleo and

clamshell rear door segments. Each main-wheel well is closed by a forward-hinged panel doubling as an airbrake and a side-hinged rear door. The airbrakes have a total area of 1.39 m² (14.9 sq ft) and open 39°.

In addition to the wheel brakes, two cruciform brake parachutes with a total area of 50 m² (537.6 sq ft) are provided to shorten the landing run; they are extracted by drag chutes each with an area of 0.05 and 1.5 m² (0.53 and 16.12 sq ft) respectively. The brake parachute container is located dorsally between the engine nozzles.

The MiG-31 is powered by two Solov'yov D30F-6S afterburning turbofans rated at 9,140-9,270 kgp (20,400-20,690 lbst) dry and 14,965-15,510 kgp (33,400-34,620 lbst)

The port fin and stabilator of an early MiG-31 *sans suffixe* (note the exposed outer petals of the engine nozzle). The fin leading edge is dielectric, housing an antenna.

The starboard fin and stabilator of a MiG-31 *sans suffixe*; note that the leading edge is metal.

reheat. The D30F-6S is a two-spool turbofan with a fixed-area subsonic air intake, a five-stage axial low-pressure (LP) compressor, a ten-stage axial high-pressure (HP) compressor, a can-annular combustion chamber with 12 flame tubes, two-stage axial HP and LP turbines (the former has air-cooled blades), an afterburner and a convergent-divergent axisymmetric supersonic nozzle. The afterburner has a core/bypass flow mixer and a ring-type flame holder. The nozzle is fully adjustable, with active control of the subsonic flow petals by means of 18 hydraulic rams and aerodynamic control of the supersonic flow petals. The divergent part of the nozzle incorporates suction relief valves to eliminate exhaust gas flow pulsations. Starting is electric.

Bypass ratio 0.55 in dry mode or 0.52 in reheat mode, overall engine pressure ratio at sea level 7.05, maximum turbine temperature 1,660°K; specific fuel consumption 0.72 kg/kgp·hr (lb/lbst·hr) in dry mode or 1.9 kg/kgp·hr in reheat mode. Engine dry weight is 2,416 kg (5,326 lb).

The engines are housed side by side in the rear fuselage, breathing through two-dimensional supersonic air intakes with movable lower lips and horizontal flow control ramps to ensure stable operation throughout the speed and altitude envelope. The ramps are controlled by the ARV-27 automatic intake control system (*avtomaht regooleerovaniya vozdokhozabornika*).

The MiG-31 has powered flight controls with irreversible hydraulic actuators throughout. Control inputs are transmitted to the actuators via push-pull rods, bellcranks and levers. The stabilators move symmetrically for pitch control and differentially to assist the ailerons in roll control. The rear cockpit features back-up controls (stick and rudder pedals) allowing the WSO to fly and land the aircraft. An SAU-155MP automatic control system (autopilot) is provided.

Internal fuel is carried in 13 integral tanks – seven in the fuselage (Nos. 1 and 2, frames 4-6; No. 3, frames 6-7; Nos. 4 and 5, frames 7-11; Nos. 6 and 7, frames 11-12B), four in the wings and two in the fins. Total internal fuel capacity is 18,500 litres (4,070 Imp gal); two 2,500-litre (550 Imp gal) drop tanks can be carried on the inboard wing pylons, increasing the total capacity to 23,500 litres (5,170 Imp gal). Normally the aircraft carries 13,700 litres (3,014 Imp gal) of fuel in the Nos. 2-5 fuselage tanks, the wing tanks and half-filled drop tanks. A single-point pressure refuelling connector is located in the port mainwheel well. The MiG-31 *sans suffixe* (*izdeliye* 01DZ) and MiG-31B are equipped with a probe-and-drogue IFR system, featuring a fully retractable refuelling probe offset to port ahead of the cockpit windshield.

The avionics and equipment include a weapons control system, a flight/navigation suite and a communications suite. The MiG-31 *sans suffixe* has an S-800 Zaslon *weapons control system*; it is capable of

Opposite page:
The nose landing gear unit of a MiG-31, showing the twin landing lights and the smaller taxi light built into the nose gear door.

Rear view of the nose gear, showing the tight-fitting mudguard. The port main gear door/airbrake is visible; note the integrated step for maintenance access to the equipment in the wheel well.

The starboard main gear unit, showing the bogie with its rocking damper/tilt actuator.

This page:
The R-33 missiles under the belly of a MiG-31; the forward pair is semi-recessed.

The rear pair of R-33s; note the folding upper rudders.

The R-40TD is part of the MiG-31's weapons range.

detecting targets flying at 50-30,000 m (164-98,425 ft) and up to 3,700 km/h (2,300 mph). Detection range for a bomber-sized target is 180-200 km (111-124 miles) in head-on mode and 60-80 km (37-50 miles) in pursuit mode; for a fighter-type target with an RCS of 3 m² (32.25 sq ft) it is 120-130 and 45-60 km (74.5-80.75 and 28-37 miles) respectively. The WCS enables engagement of aerial targets singly or in a group of interceptors in GCI, airborne guidance and autonomous modes, controlling the actions of aircraft in a group from the group leader's aircraft and uploading target data from the group leader's aircraft to an automated ground control system.

The WCS includes a target search/track subsystem with radar and IR channels, a weapons selector subsystem and weapons interface modules. The former subsystem is built around an RP-31 (N007, aka Model 8B 'Leningrad') fire control radar featuring a Model B01.01M monobloc phased-array antenna of 1.1 m (3 ft 7⁵⁄₁₆ in) diameter with rapid electronic beam scanning and search/track/IFF channels. The field of view is ±70° (±120° in certain modes) in azimuth and +70°/–60° in elevation; hence the radar has look-down/shoot-down capability – also against targets incorporating stealth technology, helicopters and cruise missiles. The radar can track ten targets while guiding missiles to four priority threats. The infrared channel is represented by the Model 8TK IRST housed in a retractable pod under the forward fuselage. Its field of view is ±60° in azimuth and +6°/–13° in elevation; Target detection range in pursuit mode against a fighter-type target is 40 km (24.8 miles).

Target data is processed by a digital computing system built around the A-15 'Argon-15' mainframe computer. The target indication system comprises a PPI-70V head-up display (*pilotazhno-pritsel'nyy indikahtor* – flight/sighting display) and a small ITO-1 tactical situation display (*indikahtor takticheskoy obstanovki*) in the pilot's cockpit, a larger ITO-2 display and a dual radar/IRST channel display in the WSO's cockpit.

The MiG-31B and MiG-31BS have an upgraded S-800A Zaslon-A WCS built around the RP-31A radar.

The *flight and navigation suite* includes the SAU-155MP automatic flight control system with the SOS-3M-2 flight mode limit indication system (*sistema ogranichitel'nykh signahlov*) and the KN-25 integrated navigation system. The latter enables the MiG-31 to operate in the Arctic regions lacking ground navigation aids; it includes a duplicated IS-1-72A INS, a Manyovr-V (Manoeuvre-V) digital processor, an A-312-10 Radikal-NP or a A-331 SHORAN system, an A-723 Kvitok-2 LORAN system (installed from the outset on the MiG-31/*izdeliye* 01DZ and retrofitted to the MiG-31BS), an SVS-2Ts-1 air data system (*sistema vozdooshnykh signahlov*), **Tropik** and *Marshroot* (Route) LORAN systems with an error margin of 0.13-1.3 km (0.08-0.8 miles) over a 2,000-km (1-240-mile)

Opposite page:

Top: An R-40TD on the port inboard pylon of MiG-31 '374 White'.

Upper: An APU-60-2 twin missile rail on an operational MiG-31.

Lower and bottom: Pairs of R-60M AAMs can be carried on APU-60-2 rails on the inboard pylons.

This page:

The GSh-6-23M six-barrel cannon with the rear part of the fairing removed for maintenance.

Oddly echoing early 20th century Maxim machine-guns, here the GSh-6-23M cannon with its 260-round drum is shown on a ground handling dolly.

Here the avionics bay covers are open for maintenance, showing the avionics modules inside.

The open brake parachute housing.

The 8TK IRST pod in the retracted position.

The K-36DM ejection seats of a MIG-31, marked 'front cockpit' (foreground) and 'rear cockpit'.

stage and 1.8-3.6 km (1.1-2.2 miles) over a 10,000-km (6,210-mile) stage respectively, an A-312-09 Radikal-OVK relative position assessment/formation-keeping system for group operations, a PA-4-3 automatic moving map display and so on. The flight and navigation avionics also include an ARK-19 automatic direction finder, an RV-15 (A-031) radio altimeter and an A-611 marker beacon receiver.

The *communications equipment* includes an R-862 UHF radio, an R-864 HF radio, an R-855UM radio, an SPU-9 intercorn, an 11B6 GCI command link system on MiG-31s *sans suffixe*/*izdeliye* 01 (up to and including Batch 81) or 11G6 Spektr (Spectrum) command link system on the IFR-capable *izdeliye* 01DZ (from Batch 82 onwards) and the MiG-31BS, an APD-518 secure tactical information exchange system and an RK-RLDN secure digital data link system for interaction with ground command posts.

The APD-518 works via the Radikal-NP SHORAN system, allowing information exchange within a flight of three or four MiG-31s, between the leader and the wingman in a pair, between the leaders of two or more flights, or uploading of information from a solitary interceptor to the automated ground control system. A P-591 audio warning device alerts the crew of dangerous flight modes and critical failures.

IFF equipment comprises an SRO-2P (*izdeliye* 6202) transponder and an SRZ-2P (*izdeliye* 6232), SRZ-2P3 or SRZ-035M (*izdeliye* 035M) interrogator; the latter model was fitted from the spring of 1991 onwards. An SO-69 ATC transponder is also fitted. *ESM equipment* comprises an SPO-15LM Beryoza-LM radar homing and warning system. *IRCM equipment* comprises UV-3A (APP-50) chaff/flare dispensers. *Data recording equipment* consists of the RIU registering/indication device (replaced by the Ekran BITE/CAS on the MiG-31B/MiG-31BS), Tester-UZL flight data recorder and MS-61 cockpit voice recorder.

The armament comprises missile and cannon armament. The primary *missile armament* option of the MiG-31 *sans suffixe* is four R-33 semi-active radar homing long-range AAMs carried in tandem pairs under the fuselage on AKU-410 pantographic ejector racks (the forward pair is semi-recessed). The R-33 has a launch weight of 480 kg (1,060 lb), including a 47-kg (103-lb) HE/fragmentation warhead, and a 'kill' range of 120 km (74.5 miles). Other missile options are three R-33s plus two R-40TD (or R-40T) medium-range IR-homing AAMs on the inboard wing pylons (the fourth R-33 is replaced by an APP 46TD guidance system pod for the R-40s), or four R-33s plus two R-60M short-range IR-homing AAMs on APU-60 (or four R-60Ms on APU-60-2 paired launch rails). The MiG-31B and MiG-31BS can carry up to four R-33S missiles with higher performance. The *cannon armament* consists of a 23-mm (.90 calibre) Gryazev/Shipunov GSh-6-23 or GSh-6-23M six-barrel Gatling cannon with 260 rounds installed in a fairing above the starboard mainwheel well. The rate of fire is 8,000 rpm and the muzzle velocity is 700 m/sec When the cannon is not in use the muzzle is closed by a door to reduce drag.

The crew rescue system features two Zvezda K-36DM Srs 2 zero-zero ejection seats.

■ MiG-31 SPECIFICATIONS

	MiG-31 (*izdeliye* 01)	MiG-31M
Length, including pitot	22.668 m (74 ft 5 in)	21.62 m (70 ft 11¾₆ in) [1]
Fuselage length	20.62m (67 ft 7⅞ in)	n.a.
Wing span	13.456 m (44 ft 2½ in)	13.656 m (44 ft 9⁴¹⁄₆₄ in)
Horizontal tail span	8.75 m (28 ft 8½ in)	n.a.
Height on ground	5.15 m (16 ft 10½ in) [2]	6.55 m (21 ft 5⅞ in) [2]
Wing area, m² (sq ft):		
including centre section/excluding LERXes	61.6 (663)	n.a.
less centre section (detachable wing panels only)	41.0 (441)	n.a.
Vertical tail area (total), m² (sq ft)	15.6 (167.9)	n.a.
Horizontal tail area, m² (sq ft)	9.82 (105.59)	n.a.
Landing gear track	3.638 m (11 ft 11⅞₂ in)	3.637 m (11 ft 11¾₆ in)
Landing gear wheelbase	7.113 m (23 ft 4 in)	7.253 m (23 ft 9³⁵⁄₆₄ in)
Empty weight, kg (lb)	21,820 (48,100)	21,900 (48,280)
Take-off weight, kg (lb):		
maximum fuel/no external stores	36,700 (80,910)	n.a.
normal (four R-33s and normal fuel)	37,100 (81,790)	n.a.
normal (four R-33s and maximum fuel)	41,000 (90,390)	45,900 (101,190)
maximum (four R-33s, max fuel and drop tanks)	46,200 (101,850)	51,500 (113,540)
Maximum landing weight, kg (lb)	26,600 (58,640)	
Fuel capacity, litres (Imp gal):		
normal internal	13,700 (3,014)	n.a.
maximum internal	18,500 (4,070)	n.a.
ditto, with drop tanks	23,500 (5,170)	n.a.
Maximum fuel load, kg (lb):		
internal	16,350 (36,045)	17,600 (38,800)
with drop tanks	20,550 (45,300)	n.a.
Thrust/weight ratio at normal take-off weight	0.76	n.a.
Wing loading at normal take-off weight, kg/m² (lb/sq ft)	666 (136)	n.a.
Cruising speed, km/h (mph):		
supersonic	2,500 (1,553)	n.a.
subsonic	900 (559)	n.a.
Maximum speed, km/h (mph):		
at sea level	1,500 (932)	n.a.
at 17,000 m (55,770 ft) and above	3,000 (1,864)	3,000 (1,864)
Maximum Mach number	2.83	2.83
Maximum Mach number with underwing stores:		
with R-40TD AAMs	2.35	2.35
with drop tanks at 10,000 m (32,810 ft)	0.9	n.a.
Unstick speed, km/h (mph):		
with a 37,100-kg take-off weight	345 (214)	n.a.
with a 41,000-kg take-off weight	365 (226)	n.a.
Landing speed at maximum landing weight, km/h (mph)	280-285 (173-177)	n.a.
Service ceiling, m (ft)	20,600 (67,585) [3]	20,000 (65,620)
Climb time to 19,000 m (62,335 ft), minutes	7.9 [4]	
Rate of climb, m/sec (ft/min):		
Option A [5]	174 (34,240)	n.a.
Option B	140 (27,550)	n.a.
Option C	115 (22,630)	n.a.
Maximum range with four R-33s, km (miles):		
at Mach 2.35	1,400 (869)	n.a.
at Mach 0.8 on internal fuel	2,150-2,400 (1,335-1,491)	n.a.
at Mach 0.8 with drop tanks	2,850-3,000 (1,770-1,864)	3,000 (1,864) [6]
Ferry range, km (miles)	3,300 (2,050)	n.a.
Intercept range, km (miles):		
supersonic	720 (447)	n.a.
subsonic, on internal fuel only	1,200 (745)	n.a.
subsonic, with drop tanks	1,400 (870)	n.a.
subsonic, with drop tanks and one refuelling	2,000 (1,242) [7]	n.a.
Endurance, hours:		
on internal fuel only	3.6	n.a.
with one refuelling	6-7 7	n.a.
G limit	5.0; 4.5; 2.5 [8]	4.3; 3.9; 3.0 [9]
Take-off run at 37,100 kg (81,790 lb), m (ft)	950 (3,120)	n.a.
Landing run at 26,600 kg (58,640 lb), m (ft)	800-900 (2,620-2,950)	n.a.

1. Less pitot; 2. Also stated as 6.15 m (20 ft 2⅛ in) for both versions; 3. With four R-33s and 2,300 kg (5,070 lb) of fuel remaining; 4. With four R-33s and normal fuel; 5. Option A, at a 31,000-kg (68,340-lb) AUW, 'clean', at 2,000 m (6,560 ft) and Mach 0.9. Option B, ditto, at 15,000 m (49,210 ft) and Mach 2.35. Option C, at a 35,000-kg (77,160-lb) AUW, with missiles, at 15,000 m and Mach 2.35; 6. Reported as 3,000 km without details of flight mode or external stores; 7. MiG-31 (izdeliye 01DZ) and MiG-31B; 8. With 6,000 kg (13,230 lb) of fuel or less; at Mach 0.8-1.5 without drop tanks; with drop tanks; 9. Below Mach 0.8; above Mach 0.8; with K-77 missiles on the wing pylons

The Modeller's Corner

Unsurprisingly, the MiG-31 is a perennially popular subject with the model kit manufacturers – it's Russian, it's military, it's high-performance! A quick survey of the kit market turns up no fewer than 29 kits in three scales from 19 (!) brands – both the major kit manufacturers (at least some of them) and the rather obscure ones, using both the traditional (high-pressure) injection moulding technology, the 'short run' technology and the vacuform technology. However, a closer look reveals that many of these kits are reboxed versions; worse, many of them have been cloned from a woefully inadequate kit.

1:48th scale

Above: The box top of the Lindberg 1:48th scale MiG-31 kit. The box art speaks for itself – it is one of the early artist's impressions of the *Foxhound*.

The first offering to this scale was an injection moulded kit by the US company **Lindberg** (Ref. No.5001). This was an early, and consequently very inaccurate, kit which did not capture the lines of the *Foxhound* at all; while the dimensions were more or less correct, the shape of just about everything was wrong (especially the nose section), the nose gear unit was depicted as forward-retracting (MiG-25 style), and the MiG-31's most distinctive features – the semi-recessed R-33 missiles and the cannon fairing – were not reproduced at all.

Somewhat later the South Korean manufacturer **ACE Hobby Kit** released a 1:48th scale kit of the MiG-31 (Ref. No.2002). However, its accuracy was obviously horrible, if the other kits of the subject from ACE Hobby Kit are any indication.

Much later another US manufacturer, **Collect-Aire Models**, released a limited edition kit of the MiG-31BM (Ref. No.4867) in their Hi-Tech series. Actually the model, which is no longer in production, was designed in the Czech Republic by the LF Company and manufactured in the USA. It is cast in polyester resin, with 34 white metal parts for the landing gear, a vacuform canopy (in three copies!) that can be cut into sections if you choose to have it open, and a photo-etched (PE) fret with 83 exterior and interior parts (although one kit review mentions 80 parts in injected grey styrene and 16 parts in cream-coloured resin). The kit appears to be quite accurate, and the surface finish is excellent, the major airframe components having finely engraved panel lines. The fuselage is in four main pieces (vertically split cockpit section-cum-radome and vertically split centre/rear fuselage); the air intakes are separate castings with boundary layer spill ducts. The wings, vertical tails and stabilators are one-piece castings. Much attention has been paid to interior detail: the cockpits have PE instrument panels and sidewalls (the instrument dials being printed on paper to go underneath), and the internal structure of the

Opposite, bottom: The Lindberg MiG-31 built by Said 'Shark' Ordaz. The kit was built pretty much 'out of the box', but a few changes were nevertheless made. All panel lines have been rescribed and rivet detail has been added. The totally inadequate stock nose gear unit (which was depicted as forward-retracting, MiG-25 style!) has been replaced by a scratchbuilt aft-retracting version; hydraulic lines have been added to all three landing gear struts, but the excessively small stock mainwheels have been retained, and no attempt has been made to correct the main gear doors-cum-airbrakes. Aftermarket K-36D ejection seats cast in resin have been used.

Right: This view of the Lindberg MiG-31 built by Said Ordaz shows the kit's belly with not even a hint of the recesses/ejector racks for the R-33 missiles.

Below: The Lindberg MiG-31 built by Armin Knes as a MiG-31BS. Actually this is more of a scratchbuilding and kit-bashing exercise; the only parts of the original kit left unmodified are the stabilators and the nosewheels! The wings have been 'doctored' to featured drooped LE and TE flaps; the wheel well doors and airbrakes have been fashioned from plastic card, the radome is scratchbuilt, and the stock one-piece canopy has been substituted with a four-piece canopy revealing the cockpit interior. The mainwheels have been taken from the OEZ Letohrad 1:48th scale Sukhoi Su-7BKL kit. The R-33S AAMs are modified versions of AIR-54 Phoenix missiles from Monogram's Grumman F-14A Tomcat kit, the R-40RD AAMs come straight from Revell's MiG-25PD kit (incidentally, they should be R-40TDs, as the MiG-31 does not carry the radar-homing version), and the PTB-2500 drop tanks are scratchbuilt.

wheel wells, gear doors and canopies is faithfully reproduced. Of course, there are a few drawbacks. For one thing, while the parts fit is generally good, the cockpit area is somewhat tricky to assemble. For another, the engine compressor faces are included (as PE parts) but the inlet ducts are not, which means either scratchbuilding the ducts or blanking the intakes off with scratchbuilt covers. Also, the brake parachute housing at the end of the fuselage spine is wider than the spine itself, which needs fixing. A full complement of R-33 and R-60M AAMs is provided but, unfortunately, not the belly-mounted ejector racks and fin accommodation slots for the former type. The assembly instructions are very clear and detailed, which helps when assembling the intricate main gear units from multiple parts, and feature five colour scheme options, including the MiG-31BM demonstrator with the striped radome. The two-part decal sheet features sets of black (?!), red and blue

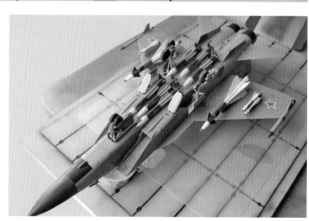

MIKOYAN
MiG-31BM
FOXHOUND

**A Rare Highly Detailed
Model of this Frontline
Russian Interceptor!**

Kit Features Fine Engraved Resin
Castings! Numerous Metal Parts!
Large Brass Photo-Engraved Sheet!
Full Accurate Cockpit! Clear Vacuform
Canopies w/Resin Inserts! Accurate,
Intricate Landing Gear! Full Missile
Load! Custom Decals For Several
Aircraft w/Full Stenciling!

*A Painstakingly Researched
Model of this Elusive Russian
Aircraft!*

HI-TECH SERIES: KIT #4867

A Custom 1/48 Scale
LIMITED EDITION KIT!

Collect-Aire Models

numerals to create any tactical code you want, lots of maintenance stencils, photo calibration markings for a development aircraft, c/ns for the missiles (rather dubious, in fact) and a very accurately reproduced individual name for a Russian Air Force aircraft – western kit manufacturers often have trouble with Cyrillic inscriptions.

Most recently, the Chinese manufacturer **AMK Hobby** (Avantgarde Model Kits) has announced a 1:48th scale injection moulded kit of the MiG-31 (Ref. No.88006) to be released in the first quarter of 2014. At the time of writing, no details are available about this kit.

1:72nd scale

Here we have a wealth of kits to choose from... or do we? The first MiG-31 kit to 1:72nd scale was probably the injection moulded kit released in the 1980s by the aforementioned **ACE Hobby Kit** (Ref. No.1037); the finished model is 320 mm (12¹⁹⁄₃₂ in) long and 86 mm (3²⁵⁄₆₄ in) tall, with a wing span of 200 mm (7⅞ in). The same manufacturer had two further kits of the MiG-31 – Ref. No.P140 (which may be an even earlier version) and Ref. No.1321. The ACE Hobby kit was extremely crude, with completely wrong contours, raised panel lines and very little detail. Yet a host of other manufacturers chose to sell reboxed versions of this kit, rather than do their own origination. These were the now-defunct South Korean manufacturer **Kitech** (Ref. No.08M-M320, sometimes reported in error as an all-new kit); **Padget** (likewise Ref. No.08M-M320); the Japanese manufacturer **Tsukuda Hobby** (Ref. No.S03, released in 1988 and also reported in error as a new kit); **Kangnam**, yet another South Korean manufacturer (Ref. No.7117, released in 2004 as a rebox of Tsukuda with new decals); the Chinese company **Zhengdefu** (Ref. No.DF320, released in 2005 as a rebox of Tsukuda with new parts); the Portuguese company **Belmonte** (likewise Ref. No.DF320, released in 2005 with different decals); and even **Revell**, which first released the kit in 1989 as Ref. No.4349 and then reissued it with different decals as Ref. No.4377 (reportedly also in 1989). (Fortunately for the German manufacturer, this was not the end of its MiG-31 story – see below.) Interestingly, many of the ACE Hobby Kit clones even featured identical, or near-identical, box art.

About the same time as the original ACE Hobby Kit release, a one-man operation in Bristol, UK, run by **Gerald J. Elliott** (he marketed the kits under his own name) released a vacuform kit of the MiG-31. The kit included white metal parts and printed instrument panels. The box was marked 'Based on available data – Not suitable for children'. This disclaimer was justified; judging by the box art, which showed a MiG-25 style undercarriage with a forward-retracting nose unit and single-wheel main units, the kit was based on the very first artist's impressions of the MiG-31 circulated in the western media and was wildly inaccurate.

The situation did not improve until 2001 when the Ukrainian manufacturer **Condor** released a reasonably accurate kit of the MiG-31 *sans suffixe* (initially as Ref. No.003). This is an injection moulded kit consisting of 107 parts cleanly moulded in light grey and clear polystyrene; the main airframe components have finely engraved panel lines. Generally the model is geometrically OK, with the exception of the fins, which are some 5° short on leading-edge sweep, and the stabilator span, which is 2 mm (0⁵⁄₆₄ in) too big. The breakdown of the kit is somewhat unusual: the entire fuselage

comes in upper and lower halves, less the air intake assemblies (which are separate parts made of two halves each), radome and rear fuselage sides. The upper fuselage half is integral with the wing centre section and upper inboard portions of the wings; the lower fuselage half features integrally moulded wheel wells (with the internal structure reproduced in the nosewheel well) and nicely done recesses with ejector racks for the R-33 missiles. The vertical tails, including the ventral fins, are moulded integrally with the rear fuselage sides, which makes sure they are splayed at the correct angle. The landing gear is reasonably well reproduced, the nose unit featuring a separate mudguard. The less-than-crystal-clear canopy comes in four parts, allowing it to be opened, but unfortunately there is not the faintest hint of the canopy frame and the periscope on the WSO's canopy. Also, the K-36D ejection seats are excellently reproduced, but otherwise the cockpit detail is sparse and warrants the use of aftermarket PE sets to pep it up a bit. External stores comprise R-33, R-40TD and R-60M AAMs, plus drop tanks. The R-40TDs are good, but the R-33s are rather too short, spoiling the impression and crying out for a replacement; the drop tanks are likewise too short, and the wing pylons are incorrect (in particular,

The early box art of the Condor 1:72nd scale MiG-31B kit.

The late box art of the Condor scale MiG-31B kit.

Opposite page:
This Lindberg MiG-31 was even more extensively rebuilt by a Russian modeller with the Internet alias Boroda ('Beard') to represent the seventh prototype MiG-31M. The original kit does have its drawbacks, but it sure beats scratchbuilding the thing from the ground up!

The box top of the Collect-Aire 1:48th scale MiG-31 kit.

This page:
The Condor MiG-31B built by Dmitriy Pavlyukov to represent MiG-31E '903 White'. The model was built pretty much 'out of the box'; panel lines were rescribed where appropriate and a few details added. The model was painted with Akan and Hobby Master paints; the distinctive pink sealant around the edges of the glazing panels was emulated with nail polish from the inside of the canopy. The decals are homemade (supplied by Yuriy Soplyachenko); after a wash of gouache and mild detergent the model was given a top coat of Akan semi-gloss varnish.

Opposite page:
The Condor MiG-31B built 'out of the box' by a modeller from Omsk with the Internet alias Zakir. Panel lines were rescribed where they were too shallow and rivet lines were added in some places. The model was painted with Zvezda enamels and given a coat of Tamiya semi-gloss acrylic varnish plus a wash of gouache and acrylic; the stock decals were complemented by stencils from the spares box.

Above: The box top of the Condor MiG-31BM kit.

Above and below: Two different versions of the box art of the ICM 1:72nd scale MiG-31 kit.

Above and below: The ICM MiG-31 built 'out of the box' by a modeller from Novosibirsk with the Internet alias Sergey. The parachutes were fashioned from papier-mâché over a modelling clay mould, using white glue, and cut to shape, using a cloth template originally meant to represent the parachutes proper, with a further coat of white glue after painting; nylon thread was used for the parachute lines.

the APU-60-2 launch rails for the R-60M missiles have a T-shaped cross-section, appearing to be *triple* rather than double!).

In 2006 Condor reissued the original MiG-31 *sans suffixe* kit with new decals as Ref. No.72009. Apart from that, reboxed versions with different decals were offered by another Ukrainian manufacturer, **ICM**, in 2005 (Ref. No.72151), as well as by two Czech companies – **MAC Distribution** in 2001 (Ref. No.72039) and **Kopro** (formerly KP, or *Kovozavody Prostějov* – Prostějov Metal Foundry) in 2004 (Ref. No.4119) – and the Polish company **Mastercraft Hobby Kits** (Ref. No.K-83).

In 2007 Condor followed up with a revised version of the kit representing the MiG-31BM (Ref. No.72011). Also in 2007, the Russian company **Eastern Express/Vostochnyy Ekspress** (best known as a 'short run' kit manufacturer) released two kits on the subject labelled MiG-31B (Ref. No.72115) and MiG-31BM (Ref. No.72116), but these are again reboxed versions of the Condor kit. The MiG-31BM kit represents the first aircraft to bear that designation (the demonstrator with strike capability) and hence includes an extra sprue with Kh-29T and Kh-31P air-to-surface missiles, R-77 AAMs and pylons for same. Regrettably, there is no Kh-58 ASM with which the demonstrator was seen at various airshows. A traditional weakness of Eastern Express is their sloppily done assembly instructions; in the case of the MiG-31BM the instructions don't even match the kit, being taken straight from the standard MiG-31B which lacks the new parts!

In 2004 the Russian manufacturer **Zvezda** (Star) hit the market with a kit of the early-production MiG-31 *sans suffixe* lacking IFR capability (Ref. No.7229). The box contains four sprues moulded in grey polystyrene and one clear sprue with a total of 119 parts. The fuselage consists of six parts – the upper/lower halves of the cockpit section/radome, the upper, lower and lateral parts of the centre/rear fuselage (the sidewalls are moulded integrally with the ventral fins). The wings and vertical tails are one-piece castings, the mainwheel wells are separate parts; somewhat unusually, the nose gear mudguard is in two halves moulded *integrally with the nosewheels*. This time the canopy (again moulded in four pieces) has the framing reproduced and even the rear cockpit periscope; unfortunately the latter cannot be modelled in the deployed position. The good news is that the model is more accurate than the Condor kit. On the minus side, the parts fit leaves something to be desired and the panel lines are decidedly overdone;

This page: The ICM MiG-31 built by Aleksey Antipin to represent MiG-31E '903 White'. The build was a two-stage process – first the model was slapped together rather hastily to meet a deadline for a competition and then various details, which were substandard, had to be corrected. The cockpits were upgraded during Stage 1, using the Part PE set and NeOmega K-36DM ejection seats; the cockpit interior was painted with Akan turquoise enamel, while the sealant on the canopy glazing was reproduced by spraying the masked canopy with pink before applying the upper coat of black. The wheel wells' internal detail was sanded down and redone (the corrugated walls were emulated with embossed tin foil) and Elf resin/rubber wheels were used; the afterburners were modified, using PE parts left over from a Hasegawa Sukhoi Su-27 kit. The model was painted with Akan enamels and finished with decals from the Begemot set. During Stage 2 the substandard gear doors were remanufactured, the insides of the movable canopy sections were revised, various missing external sensors were added and the model was given a slight wash for added realism.

Above and right: The ICM MiG-31 built by Yuriy Soplyachenko to represent a 174th GvIAP/Sqn 1 aircraft – the first to wear the tactical code '08 Red' and the name 'Boris Safonov' (c/n N69700118127) in 1982. The model was built 'out of the box' and painted with Tamiya acrylic paints; Condor decals were used. Tamiya pigments were used for weathering, with wash (gouache and detergent) and a top coat of Tamiya TS-80 matt varnish.

Below: The Eastern Express 1:72nd scale MiG-31B kit – note the 'Runglish' spelling of the reporting name; and the Eastern Express 1:72nd scale MiG-31BM kit.

Top left: The box top of the Zvezda 1:72nd scale MiG-31 kit.

Above and left: The Zvezda MiG-31 *sans suffixe* '31 Blue' built 'out of the box' by Ignat Pomazkov, with preshading and post-shading; for want of a suitable 'gun metal' paint the engine nozzles were rubbed with graphite from a lead pencil! Note the MiG logos applied back to front by mistake; the missiles are painted without much regard for realism.

The Zvezda MiG-31 *sans suffixe* '99 Blue' built by Vladimir Kuz'min to represent a 530th IAP aircraft with the distinctive killer whale nose art. Rivet detail was added, the main gear units were reinforced, the stock wheels and landing/taxi lights were substituted with aftermarket items by Elf; the R-33 missiles' proximity fuse aerials and the chrome plating on the oleo struts were reproduced with metal foil. R-73 AAMs and their launch rails by ICM were added. The model was painted with Tamiya acrylic paints; Begemot decals were used, with a top coat of Tamiya TS-80 matt varnish and wash (gouache and detergent); Tamiya pigments were used for weathering. The model was painted with Tamiya acrylic paints and Begemot decals were used; this was followed by the use of MiG wash, Tamiya pigments for weathering, highlighting of panel lines with a lead pencil and, finally, a top coat of Tamiya semi-matt varnish.

Top left: The box top of the Zvezda 1:72nd scale MiG-31B kit.

Above and left: The Zvezda MiG-31B '74 Blue' built 'out of the box' by a modeller with the Internet alias Artyom.

Right: The Zvezda MiG-31B '04 Blue' built by Yufei Mao in 2008 to represent a 712th IAP aircraft from Kansk. Modifications included scratchbuilding the air intakes and adding nozzle shrouds fabricated from thin plastic sheet to represent the late production version; the afterburner flame holders were also scratchbuilt. The cockpits were completed with the Part PE set and NeOmega resin K-36DM seats, and the canopy was modified. Landing gear detail was added, as were resin R-60M AAMs from Tally-Ho! on scratchbuilt APU-60-2 launch rails. The model was finished with Begemot decals. The ladders and wheel chocks are from a PE set by Flightpath. The figures are modified from the Luftwaffe air/ground crew set by Preiser (Ref. No.72520).

Opposite page: The new Revell 1:72nd scale MiG-31B kit – a rebox of the Zvezda kit.

The Revell MiG-31B built 'out of the box' by Thomas Berger to represent a Russian Air Force/458th GvIAP aircraft named 'Zakhar Sorokin' (c/n N69700125846) which was damaged beyond repair in February 2001.

The Revell MiG-31B built by Sven Modrzik to represent a Russian Air Force/786th GvIAP aircraft (c/n N38401208918). The model is built 'out of the box', with the addition of wheel well detail and the inner nozzle petals fashioned from plastic card; preshading with an Edding 8400 No.1 black marker has been used.

The box top of the Revell 1:144th scale MiG-31 kit.

another grievance concerns the quality of the decals, which tend to fall apart when being transferred. Speaking of decals, the instruction sheet gives two colour scheme options, one of which is a grey/blue/white demonstrator aircraft coded '374 White'; however, this colour scheme does not fit the kit because '374 White' does have IFR capability!

In 2005 Zvezda reissued the kit with new parts as the MiG-31B (Ref. No.7244), increasing the number of parts to 128; the decal sheet featured options for two Russian Air Force aircraft in standard grey colours and a further demonstrator in the abovementioned grey/blue/white scheme coded '903 White'. As in the Condor kit, the IFR probe and the IRST unit are separate parts, but they can only be modelled in the retracted position. This kit was reboxed by **Revell** in 2006 (Ref. No.04378) and by **ICM** in 2008; despite being a new kit with different tooling, the ICM version ostensibly (and confusingly) has the same reference No.72151 as the ex-Condor version, so watch out.

1:144th scale

Choice is limited to a single kit by **ACE Hobby Kit** (Ref. No.1015), which was later reboxed by **Revell** as Ref. No.04086. It is a scaled-down version of the 1:72nd scale kit, and consequently inherits all of its inaccuracies, including the MiG-25 style landing gear.

AFTERMARKET ITEMS

Add-ons for those who wish to add realism to their MiG-31 model are surprisingly few. Thus, just about the only aftermarket item in **1:48th scale** is the K-36DM ejection seat available from a number of resin kit/accessories manufacturers – the Russian company **NeOmega** (Ref. No.48E04), the Czech companies **Pavla Models** (Ref. No.S48007) and **AiRes** (with PE parts, Ref. No.4054), the US company **Verlinden Productions** (Ref. No.VERL.636), **FM Detail Sets** (Ref. No.480805), **Wolfpack** (Ref. No.WP48106), **Ciro Models** (Ref. No.C-423), **True Details** (Ref. No.TD48404), **Sol Models** (Ref. No.MM057) and probably others. Actually this item is not 'Foxhound-specific', being the standard Soviet ejection seat, and thus is offered for various Russian aircraft kits (the MiG-29, Su-27, Su-25 and Su-34).

In **1:72nd scale**, two Russian companies – **Equipage** and **NeOmega** – offer sets of resin/rubber wheels for the MiG-31. In 2008 the Russian company **EdModels** released a photo-etched parts set for the ICM kit (though the inevitable question arises: *which* kit, the old one or the new one?). The set (Ref. No.ERU72005) was the Czech company **Eduard Models**, with their usual high quality standard, and features pitots, aerials, rudder pedals, pre-painted (and very realistic) instrument panels, cockpit sidewalls and seat harness. The seat belts are of the wrong colour; while this shortcoming is easily remedied by repainting, a more serious omission is the almost complete lack of canopy interior detail, such as the famous periscope.

Two further PE parts sets are available from the Polish accessories supplier **Part**. The first of these (Ref. No.S72-148) is a cockpit set comprising the instrument panels and their shrouds, ejection seat details and rudder pedals. The other (Ref. No.73356) is an exterior set consisting of two PE frets with the wing fences, mainwheel disc faces, fins for the R-33 and R-40TD AAMs, pitots and the like. Once again, K-36DM seats in resin are offered by a host of manufacturers – **NeOmega** (Ref. No.E4), **Heritage Aviation** (Ref. No.HAAC72013), **Verlinden Productions** (Ref. No.VERL.648), **True Details** (Ref. No.TD72401), **Wolfpack** (Ref. No.WP72042) and so on.

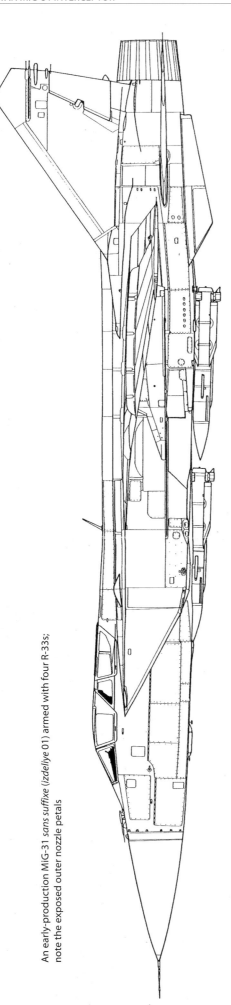

An early-production MiG-31 *sans suffixe (izdeliye 01)* armed with four R-33s; note the exposed outer nozzle petals

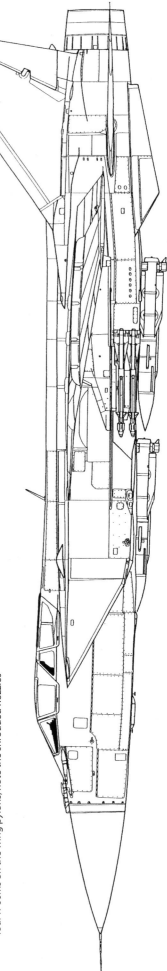

An IFR-capable MiG-31 *sans suffixe (izdeliye 01DZ)* armed with four R-33s and four R-60Ms on the wing pylons; note the shrouded nozzles

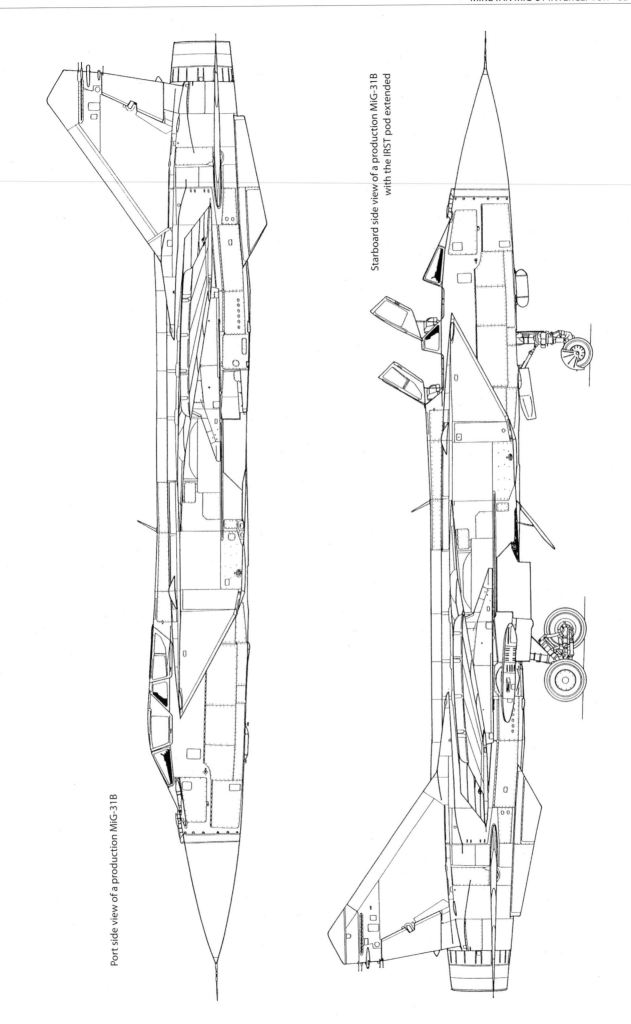

Starboard side view of a production MiG-31B
with the IRST pod extended

Port side view of a production MiG-31B

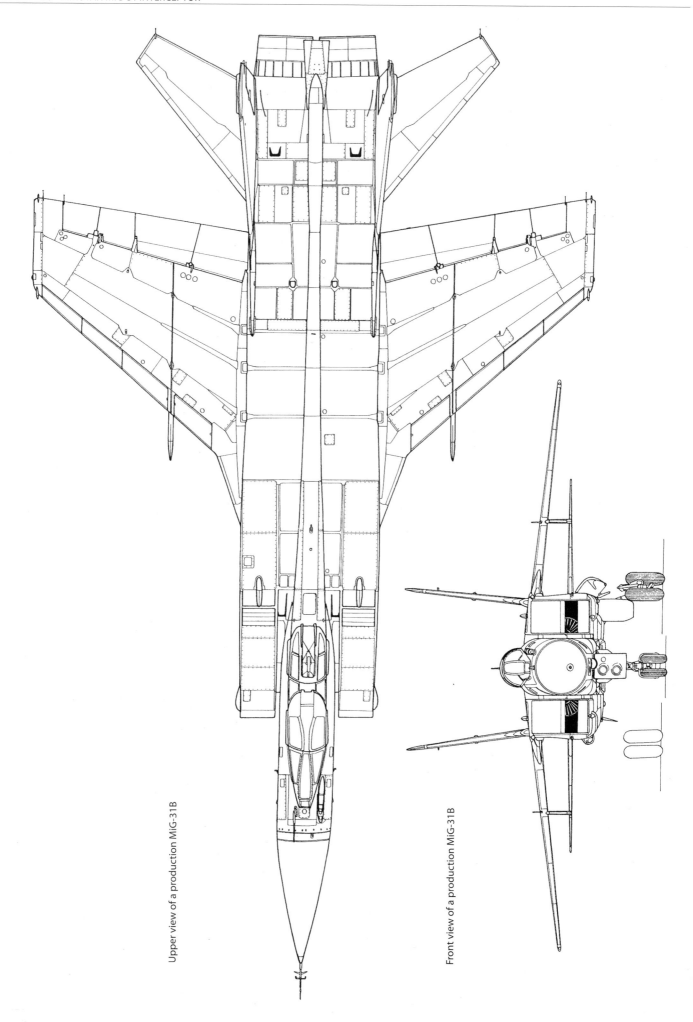

Upper view of a production MiG-31B

Front view of a production MiG-31B

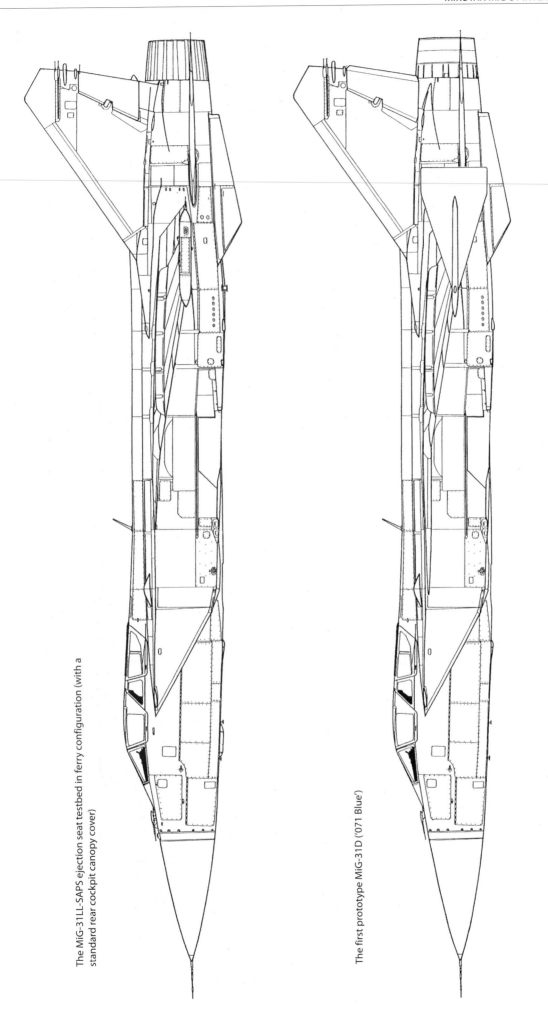

The MiG-31LL-SAPS ejection seat testbed in ferry configuration (with a standard rear cockpit canopy cover)

The first prototype MiG-31D ('071 Blue')

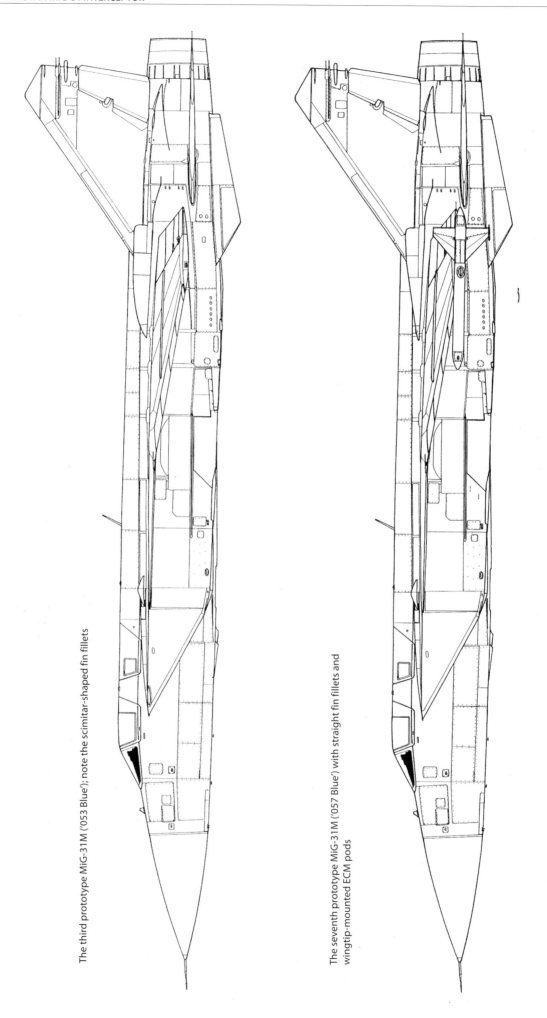

The third prototype MiG-31M ('053 Blue'); note the scimitar-shaped fin fillets

The seventh prototype MiG-31M ('057 Blue') with straight fin fillets and wingtip-mounted ECM pods

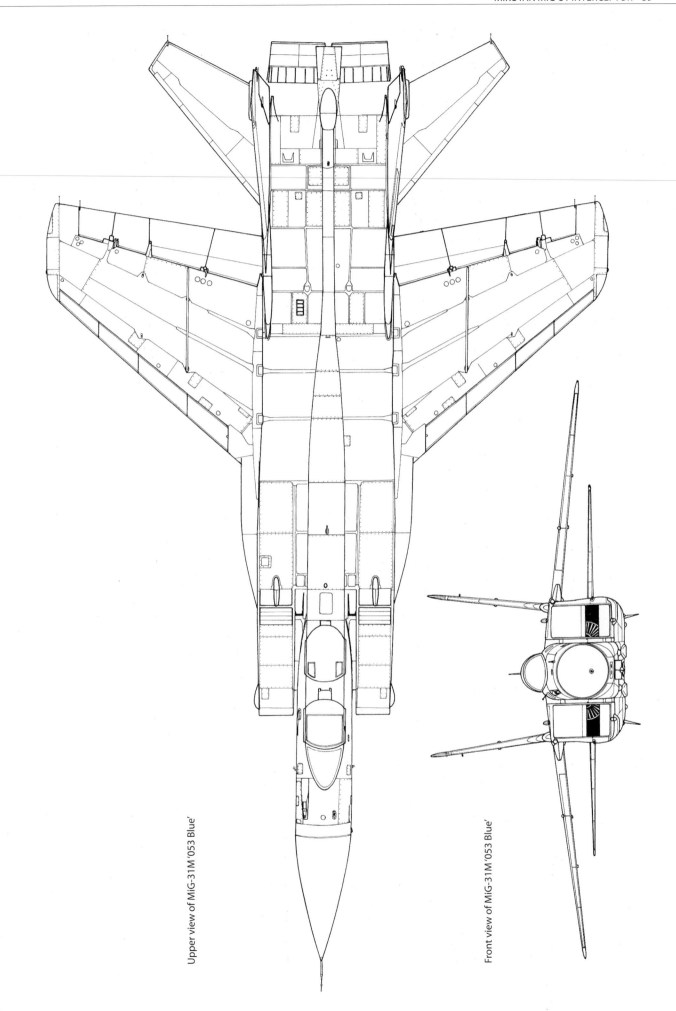

Upper view of MiG-31M '053 Blue'

Front view of MiG-31M '053 Blue'

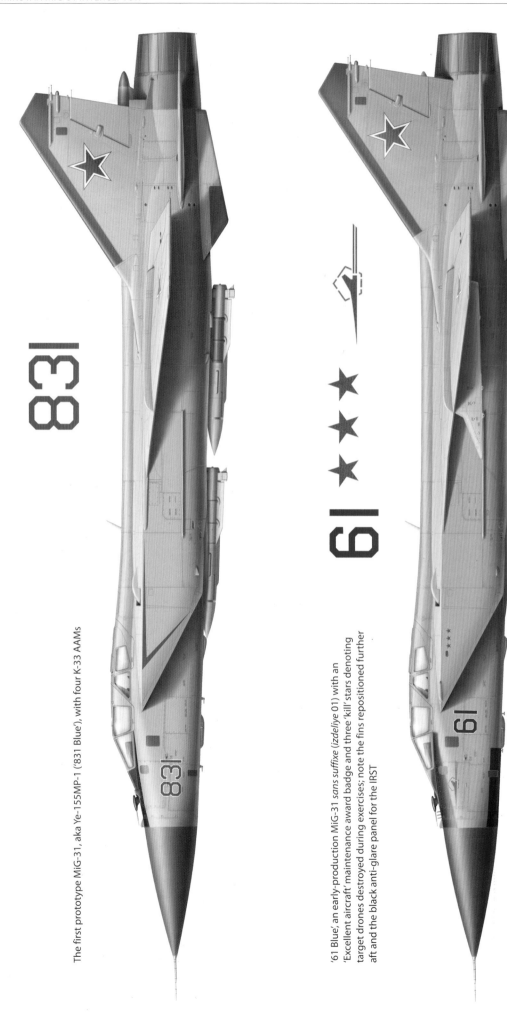

The first prototype MiG-31, aka Ye-155MP-1 ('831 Blue'), with four K-33 AAMs

'61 Blue', an early-production MiG-31 *sans suffixe* (*izdeliye* 01) with an 'Excellent aircraft' maintenance award badge and three 'kill' stars denoting target drones destroyed during exercises; note the fins repositioned further aft and the black anti-glare panel for the IRST

MiG-31 *sans suffixe* (*izdeliye* 01) '84 Red' (c/n N69700125578) named 'Vasiliy Strel'nikov' (a Hero of the Soviet Union, as indicated by the Gold Star Medal), 458th GvIAP, Savvatiya AB, Kotlas; the other inscription reads 'Guards Fighter Regiment named after [Boris F.] Safonov'

MiG-31 *sans suffixe* (*izdeliye* 01DZ) '10 Red' with a locally applied Mikoyan OKB logo and APU-60-2 paired missile rails on the wing pylons

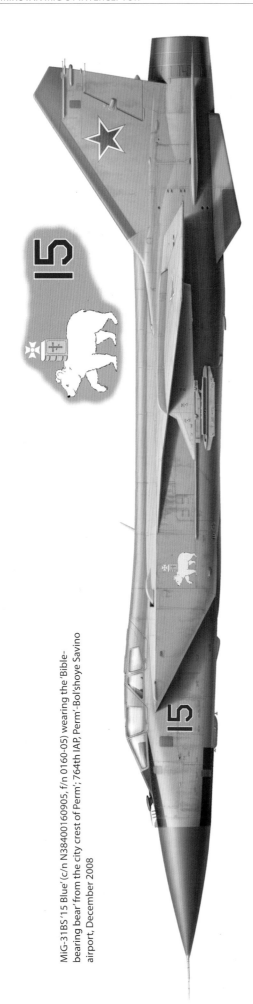

MiG-31BS '15 Blue' (c/n N38400160905, f/n 0160-05) wearing the 'Bible-bearing bear' from the city crest of Perm'; 764th IAP, Perm'-Bol'shoye Savino airport, December 2008

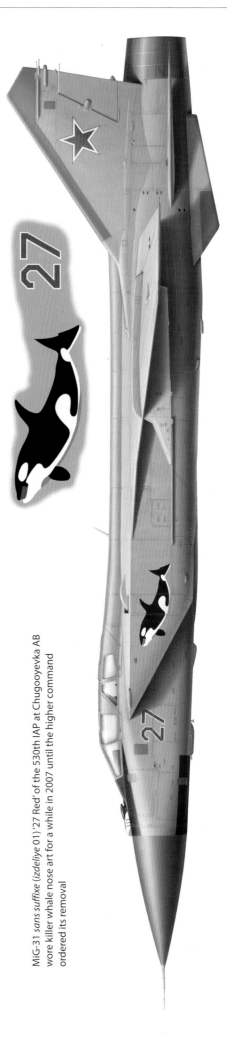

MiG-31 sans suffixe (izdeliye 01) '27 Red' of the 530th IAP at Chugooyevka AB wore killer whale nose art for a while in 2007 until the higher command ordered its removal

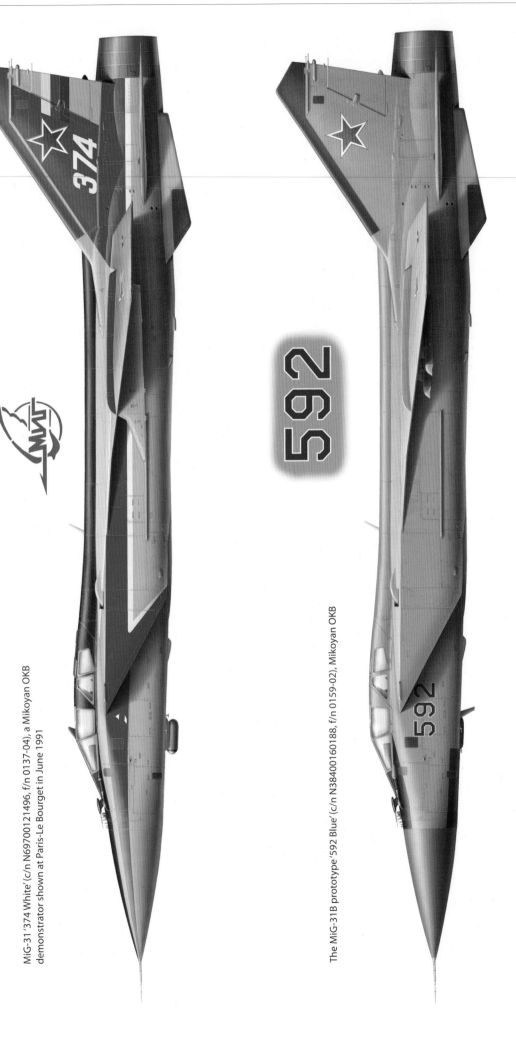

MiG-31 '374 White' (c/n N69700121496, f/n 0137-04), a Mikoyan OKB demonstrator shown at Paris-Le Bourget in June 1991

The MiG-31B prototype '592 Blue' (c/n N3840016O188, f/n 0159-02), Mikoyan OKB

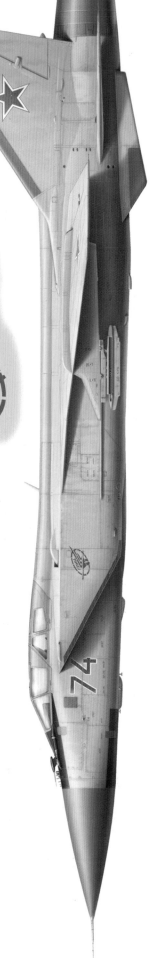

'74 Red' (c/n N38400181345, f/n 0182-01), the first production MiG-31 *sans suffixe* (*izdeliye* 01DZ), 929th GLITs, Akhtoobinsk; note the Centre's logo on the air intake

The MiG-31LL-SAPS ejection seat testbed (c/n N6970011 6548) belonging to GNIKI VVS in operational configuration with the rear cockpit canopy removed and a slipstream deflector fitted, 1992; note the 'bald lion' nose art hinting at the testbed role

MiG-31BS '22 Blue'/RF-95444 of the 6980th AvB/2nd AvGr at Perm'-Bol'shoye Savino was christened 'Permskiy Kray' (Perm'Territory) on 7th November 2012

MiG-31BM '29 Red'/RF-90886 named 'Viktor Shlyopov' (HSU), 6980th AvB/3rd AvGr, Kansk-Dal'niy AB, 2013

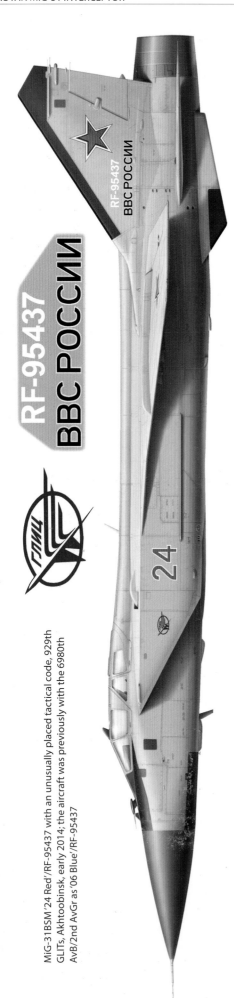

RF-95437
ВВС РОССИИ

MiG-31BSM '24 Red'/RF-95437 with an unusually placed tactical code, 929th GLITs, Akhtoobinsk, early 2014; the aircraft was previously with the 6980th AvB/2nd AvGr as '06 Blue'/RF-95437

Kazakhstan Air Force MiG-31 sans suffixe (izdeliye 01) '21 Red', 610th Aviation Base, Sary-Arka AB, Qaragandy (Karaganda); the unit badge on the air intake features the Kazakh acronym KRKK standing for 'Republic of Kazakhstan Armed Forces'